New Familiar
Abenakis and
English Dialogues

New Familiar Abenakis and English Dialogues

The First Vocabulary Ever Published in the Abenakis Language

Abenakis Chief
Joseph Laurent

MINT EDITIONS

New Familiar Abenakis and English Dialogues: The First Vocabulary Ever Published in the Abenakis Language was first published in 1884.

This edition published by Mint Editions 2023.

ISBN 9798888970027 | E-ISBN 9798888970171

Published by Mint Editions®

MINT EDITIONS

minteditionbooks.com

Publishing Director: Katie Connolly
Design: Ponderosa Pine Design
Production and Project Management: Micaela Clark
Typesetting: Westchester Publishing Services

Contents

Preface

The primary intention, the chief aim of the Editor in publishing this book, is to aid the young generation of the Abenakis tribe in learning English.

It is also intended to preserve the *uncultivated* Abenakis language from the gradual alterations which are continually occurring from want, of course, of some proper work showing the grammatical principles upon which it is dependent. Hence the many remarks and explanations which are to be found all through this book: *ciphers, italics, etc., etc.,* employed in view to extend its utility.

As no pains have been spared to render as easy as possible the learning of the pronunciation, and the signification of every Indian word inserted in this book, and that the Abenakis language contains no articulations that the English vocal organs are not accustomed to, the writer hopes that many of the white people will be glad to avail themselves of the advantage and facility thus afforded to them for becoming acquainted in some measure, and with very little trouble, with that truly *admirable* language of those Aborigines called *Abenakis,* which, from the original word *Wôbanaki,* means: peasant or inhabitant from the East.

May this little volume, which will learn the white man how the Abenakis vocal organs express God's attributes, the names of the various objects of the creation: beasts, birds, fishes, trees, fruits, etc., etc., and how extended are the modifications of the Abenakis verb, be welcomed by the white as well as by the red man, and its errors and defects overlooked with indulgence.

Sozap Lolô, *alias,*
Jos. Laurent.

The Abenakis Alphabet

Aa	Bb	Cc	Dd
Ee	Gg	Hh	Ii
Jj	Kk	Ll	Mm
Nn	Oo	(O'ô, nasal)	
Pp	Ss	Tt	Uu
	Ww	Zz	

Vowels

Aa   Ei   Ii   Oo   (O'ô)   Uu

Diphthongs

ai   ao   aô   ia   io   iô

iu   ua   ue   ui   uô

SYLLABLES

in progressive scale

1. a   i   o   ô   u
2. ba bi bo da do dô ga hi jo kô la me ni po sô ta wô zo
3. ban den gin jôn kas les mon nôp hla (or lha) taw môw ton gua gai kuô kwa gui pia wia
4. dagw makw guôn kwôn mska kigw ngue tegw tukw skua chan chiz
5. laskw gaskw pskwa lhagw pkuam pkwak wzukw wskit
6. bapskw gapskw sipskw lhakws mskagw lômskw

Words and Syllables

1. Monosyllables. *U,* here; *ti*, tea; *moz,* moose; *sen,* stone; *sibs,* duck; *skog,* snake; *kôgw,* porcupine.

2. Dissyllables. *A-bôn,* cake, *si-bo,* river; *nol-ka,* deer; *môlsem,* wolf; *wô-boz,* elk; *A-kigw,* seal.

3. Trisyllables. *Sa-no-ba,* man; *Al-nô-ba,* Indian; *pas-to-ni,* American; *pa-po-les,* whip-poor-will; *pskwa-sa-wôn,* flower.

4. Polysyllables. *A-bôn-kô-gan,* oven; *kio-da-win-no,* traveler; *pô-ba-tam-win-no,* a christian; *wi-ges-mo-win-no,* drunkard; *a-ia-mi-ha-wi-ga-migw,* church, (*lit. meaning:* house of prayer).

KEY OF THE PRONUNCIATION

The *fifteen consonants* of the Abenakis Alphabet are sounded, as in English, *b, d* final being always sounded respectively, as *p, t: Azib,* sheep (azip); *Tabid,* David, (Tabit).

G is always *hard* as in *good, begin: pego,* gum; *tego,* wave.

The *joined* letters *ch* have a *lingual-dental* sound, that is to say softer (more slender) than *ch* in the English words *chin, watch: chibai,* ghost; *chiga?* when?

I is sounded like *ch: Kabij,* cabbage, (kabich).

Ph must not be sounded as *f,* because this letter is not in use in the Abenakis language. Thus, *phanem,* woman, must be articulated nearly as if its proper orthography was *pe-ha-nem,* expressed in two syllables (p'ha-nem), with an aspirate sound to the first, owing to the presence of *h,* which is always more or less aspirated.

All the consonants must be sounded: *namas,* fish; *môlsem,* wolf; *abon,* bed. There is no exception.

When a consonant (so as a vowel) is *doubled*—thus: *.bb, nn, tt*—the two letters are to be sounded as one, the sound being *prolonged;* as in the following sentence: *n'winowôziibba nitta,* I should have petitioned forthwith.

The Vowels are sounded as in the following scale:

A as in *master: abaznoda,* basket;

E as in *label: pelaz,* pigeon;

I as in *indian: liguônsôgan,* thimble;

O as in *notice:* todosnôbo, milk;

U is sounded as *u* in *union:* 1. When it occurs alone; 2. When it is first in a word; 3. When it is preceded by *i: u nia,* this is mine; *ulil niuna,* these are ours. But when *u* is preceded by a consonant other than *g* or *k,* it is sounded like *e* (Abenakis). Thus we could as well articulate *niben,* summer, by *ni-bun.*

The diphthongs are sounded thus:

Ai as *i* in *wine: n'-d-ain,* I am present;

Ao as *o* in *how: chilao,* he (she) is cross;

la as *ia* in *asiatic: nia,* me, to me, I, mine;

Io, iu as *eo* in geometric: *wios,* meat, flesh; *niuna,* us, to us, we, our, ours;

Ua, ue, ui, uô, as *wa, we, wi, wô,* (in Abenakis): *taguahôgan,* mill; *kwikueskas,* robin; *kwiguigem,* black duck; *saguôlhigan,* ramrod, (*analogous sound:* ta-gwahôgan, kui-kwes-kas, kui-gwi-gem, sa-gwôl-higan).

Aô, iô, nasal diphthongs, are sounded in the same scale as *ao, io,* (distinct articulation of vowels in one syllable) e. g. *pa-iô,* arrive.

VOCABULARY

OF GOD'S ATTRIBUTES.

Kchi Niwaskw.	God, The Great Spirit.
Niwaskowôgan.	Deity.
Niwaskw.	Spirit.
Wanamônit.	The Father.
Wamitôgwsit.	The Son.
Wiji-Wliniwaskwit.	The Holy Ghost.
Nasichebikinawsit.	The Trinity.
Tabaldak.	The Lord.
Nônguichi-Ntatôgw.	The Almighty.
Nônguitegilek.	The Omnipotent.
Askaminnowit.	The Eternal.
Kdemôgaldowôgan.	Mercy.
Sasaginnowôgan.	Justice, Perfection.
Sazos.	Jesus-Christ.
Polwakhowawinno.	The Saviour.
Alnôbaiosowôgan.	The Incarnation.
Mamagahodwôgan.	The Passion.
Sidakwtahodwôgan.	The Crucifixion.
Polwakhowawôgan.	The Redemption.
Spemkik Alihlôd.	The Ascension.
Polwawôgan.	Salvation.
Lôgitôwadwôgan.	Adoration.
Pôbatamwôgan.	Religion.
Wlômawaldamwôgan.	Faith.
Nkawatzowôgan.	Hope.
Kdemôgalgawôgan.	Charity.

OF THE HEAVENS.

Spemki.	Heaven, Paradise.
Asokw.	Firmament, sky, cloud.
Kakasakw.	Blue sky; starry heaven.
O'zali.	An angel.
Kchi ôzali.	An archangel.

Sôgmôwi Mali.	The Virgin Mary.
" "	The Holy Virgin.
Wawasinno.	A saint, a blessed.
Mjejakw.	A soul.
Wli mjejakw.	A blessed soul.
Wdawasgiskwi.	An apostle.
Wawasi kigamowinno.	An evangelist.
Kisos.	The sun; moon; month.
Pôgwas, nahnibôssat.	The moon.
Alakws.	A star.
Kchi alakws.	The morning, or evening star.
Pili kisos.	New moon.
Pôguasek.	Moon light.
Managuôn.	A rainbow.

OF THE ELEMENTS AND THINGS RELATING TO THEM.

Awan.	Air.
Kzelômsen.	The wind; it blows.
Wlelômsen.	A gentle breeze.
"	A fresh wind; fair wind.
Kisokw.	The weather; day;
Wlekisgad.	Fair or fine weather.
Majekisgad.	Bad weather; it is—.
Soglônkisgad.	Rainy weather; it is—.
Wdagkisgad.	Wet weather, it is—.
Tka, or tkekisgad.	Cold weather; it is—.
Wlôda.	Warm weather; it is—.
Nebi.	Water.
Solgônbi.	Rain water.
Sibobi.	River water.
Tkebi.	Spring water.
Whawdazibôminebi.	Well water.
Nbisonbi,[1]. 5	Mineral water.
Pibganbi.	Muddy water.

---

1. The *ciphers* set opposite some nouns, in different parts of this book, mark the order of the plural termination to which each noun belongs; those terminations being: 1, *ak;* 2, *ik;* 3, *ok;* 4, *k;* 5, *al;* 6, *il;* 7, *ol;* 8, *l.*

Sobagw.	7	The sea, ocean.
Mamili sobagua.		The open sea, the high sea;
Wisawôgamak.	6	A strait; in the—, at the—.
Senojiwi.		The bank, the shore.
Nebes, (——ek)	5	A lake; (at, to the—).
Nebessis.	5	A pond.
Wôljebagw.	7	A marsh.
Sibo, (tegw, ttegw).	5	A river.
Sibosis.	5	A brook, stream.
Panjahlôk.	6	A cascade, a waterfall.
Pôntegw.	7	A rapid.
Kchi pôntegw.	7	A grand rapid.
Tego*ak*.		The waves.
Ki, *or* Kdakinna.		The earth; the globe.
Towipegw.		Dust.
Pegui.		Sand.
Senômkol.		Gravel.
Azesko.		Mud.
Senis.		A pebble.
Sen.		A stone.
Masipskw.		A flint.
Mskoda.		A plain.
Wajo, (aden).		A mountain.
Kajigapskw.		A steep rock.
Kôkajigapskw.	7	An extended steeprock.
Menahan.	7	An island.
Senojisobagwa.		The seacoast.
Skweda.		Fire, flame.
Ohekelas.	1	Spark.
Pekeda.		Smoke.
Wiboda.		Soot.
Skwedaipegui.		Ashes.

It must be observed, however, that the second termination (ik) requires always, before its annexation to the noun, the change of the final *d* or *t* into *j*: *Kabhôzit*, prisoner, pl. *Kabhôzijik*; (*notkuaag*, pilot, pl. *notkuaagik*).

The final letter *w* in *gw, kw*, must be suppressed before the annexation of the 7th termination (ol).

METEORS, SHIPS, ETC.

Wlôda.		Heat; there is—.
Tka.		Cold; it is—.
Tkawansen.		Cool air; it is cool.
Pakwsatakisgad.		Dry weather; it is—.
Wdagkisgad.		Damp weather; it is—.
Awan.		The air; vapour, fog.
Mnasokw.		A cloud.
Pesgawan.		Foggy; it is—.
Soglôn.		Rain; it rains.
Psôn.		It snows.
Wazôli.		Snow.
Nebiskat.		Dew.
Kladen.		Frost; it is frozen.
Sikwla.		Glazed frost.
Weskata.		Thaw; it thaws.
Pkuami; pkuamiak.		Ice; icicles.
Pabadegw.	3	Hail.
Padôgi.	1	Thunder.
Nanamkiapoda.		An earthquake; there is—.
Petguelômsen.		A whirlwind; there is—.
Ktolagw.	7	A vessel; ship; frigate.
Abodes.	5	A launch, a yawl.
Pados.	5	A boat.
Stimbot.	5	A steamer.
Mdawakwam.	1	The mast.
Sibakhiganat.		The sails.
Wlokuahigan.	5	The rudder.
Pihanak.		The ropes.
Mdawagen.	7	The flag.
Wskidolagua.		The deck; on the—.
Alômolagua.		The hold; in the—.
Alômsagw.	7	Cabin, chamber.
Alômsagok.		In the cabin,—chamber.
Kaptin.	1	The captain.
Komi.	1	The clerk.
Notkuaag.	2	The pilot.

Pgoisak.	The sailors, the crew.
Nodaksit. 2	A seaman.

THE SEASONS.

Siguan.	Spring.
Siguana.	Last spring.
Nialisiguana.	A year ago last spring.
Siguaga.	Next spring.
Siguaniwi.	In spring.
Niben.	Summer.
Nibena.	Last summer.
Nialitnibena.	A year ago last summer.
Nibega.	Next summer.
Nibeniwi.	In summer.
Taguôgo.	Autumn, fall.
Taguôgua.	Last fall.
Nialitaguôgua.	A year ago last fall.
Taguôgiga.	Next fall.
Taguôgowiwi.	In fall year.
Pebon.	Winter.
Pebona.	Last winter.
Nialippona	A year ago last winter.
Peboga.	Next winter.
Peboniwi.	In winter.

THE MONTHS.

Alamikos.	January.
Piaôdagos.	February.
Mozokas.	March.
Sogalikas.	April.
Kikas.	May.
Nakkahigas.	June.
Temaskikos.	July.
Temezôwas.	August.
Skamonkas.	September.
Penibagos.	October.

Mzatanos.	November.
Pebonkas.	December.

THE DAYS OF THE WEEK.

Sanda.	Sunday.
Kizsanda.	Monday.
Nisda alokan.	Tuesday.
Nseda alokan.	Wednesday.
Iawda alokan.	Thursday.
Skawatukwikisgad.	Friday.
Kadawsanda.	Saturday.

DIVISION OF TIME.

Kisokw.	The day; a day.
Kisgadiwi.	In day time.
Tebokw.	The night.
Nibôiwi.	In the night.
Spôsowiwi.	In the morning.
Wlôgwiwi.	In the evening.
Paskua.	Noon; it is noon.
Paskuak.	At noon.
Nôwitebakad.	Midnight; it is midnight
Nôwitebakak.	At midnight.
Sôkhipozit kisos.	Sunrise; at sunrise.
Nakilhôt kisos.	Sunset, at sunset.
Pamkisgak.	Today.
Pamlôguik.	This evening.
Wlôgwa.	Yesterday.
Saba.	Tomorrow.
Achakuiwik.	The next day.
Nguedômkipoda.	An hour; one o'clock.
Pabasômkipoda.	Half an hour.
Minit.	A minute.
Pazeguen kisokw.	A day.
Nguetsanda.	A week.
Nisda sanda.	Two weeks.
Kisos, or pazeko kisos.	A month.

Waji môjassaik.	In the beginning.
Nôwiwi *or* nanôwiwi.	The middle; at the middle.
Matanaskiwi.	The end; at the end.
Nguejigaden.	One year.
Nônguejigadegi.	Annually.

MANKIND, KINDRED, ETC.

Kchai *ta* wski alnôba *	1	The father *and* the son.
Kchiphanem ta wdosa†		The mother *and* the daughter.
Alôgomômek.		The relation.
Nmitôgwes.		My father.
Kmitôgwes.		Thy father.
Wmitôgwsa.		His (her) father.
Nigawes.		My mother.
Wigawessa.		His (her) mother.
Nmahom.		My grandfather.
Nokemes.		My grandmother.
Okemessa.		His (her) grandmother.
Okemeswô.		Their grandmother.
Niswiak.		My husband; my wife.
Niswiakw.		Thy husband, thy wife.
Niswiidiji.		His wife; her husband.
Nzihlos.		My father-in-law.
Nzegues.		My mother-in-law.
Wazilmit *or* wazilmegoa		My son-in-law.
Nsem.		My daughter-in-law.
Kalnegoa.		My godfather; my godmother.
Wskinnossis.		A lad, a little boy.
Nôkskuasis.		A young little girl.
Nôjikw.		My stepfather; my uncle.
Kokemis.		My stepmother; my aunt.
Noses.		My grandson, my granddaughter.
Osessa.		His (her) grandchild.

---

* Literally: the old man and the young man.
† The old woman and her daughter.

Nijia. *a*	1	My brother; (a term peculiar to a *male*).
Nitsakaso. *b*	1	My sister; (term peculiar to a *female*).
Nidôbso.	1	My brother; (when the speaker is a *female*).
Nidôbso.	1	My sister; (when the speaker is a *male*).
Nidokan.	1	My brother, (older than I).
Nmessis.	1	My sister, (older than I).
Nichemis.	1	My brother, my sister, (younger than I).
Nnôjikw.	1	My uncle, (my father's brother).
Nzasis.	1	My uncle, (my mother's brother).
Nokem.	1	My aunt, (my father's sister).
Nokemis.	1	My aunt, (my mother's sister).
Nadôgwes.	1	My cousin, (the son of my father's sister, or of mother's brother).
Nadôgwseskua.	1	My cousin, (a term peculiar to a *male,* which signifies: cousin of mine, the daughter of my father's sister, or of my mother's brother).
Nadôgwsis.	1	My cousin (a term peculiar to a female, which signifies: cousin of mine, the daughter of my father's sister, or of my mother's brother).
Nadôgw.	1	My brother-in-law, (a term peculiar to a male, which signifies: my wife's brother, my sister husband.

---

a. *Nijia,* a term peculiar to a male, signifies also: cousin of mine, the son of my father's brother, or of my mother's sister.

† b. *Nitsakaso,* a term peculiar to a female, signifies also: cousin of mine, the daughter of my father's brother, or of my mother's sister.

Nilem.	3	My sister-in-law, (a term peculiar to a male, which signifies: my brother's wife, my wife's sister.
Nadôgw.	1	My brother-in-law, (a term peculiar to a female, which signifies: my husband's brother, my husband's sister.
Nilem.	3	My sister-in-law, (a term peculiar to a female, which signifies: my sister's husband, my brother's wife.

FUNCTIONS, HABITS, ETC.

Nasawan.	The breathing.
Msinasa*wôgan*.[1]	A sigh.
Kôgôlwa*wôgan*.	A cry; a scream.
Nakwhômo*wôgan*.	Sneezing.
Chachapsolo*wôgan*.	The hiccough, hiccup.
Nolmukwso*wôgan*.	Drowsiness.
Chigualakwso*wôgan*.	Snoring.
Leguaso*wôgan*.	A dream.
Lalômo*wôgan*.	The voice.
Kelozo*wôgan*.	Speech.
Ladaka*wôgan*,	Gesture; action.
Wligo*wôgan*.	Beauty; goodness.
Majigo*wôgan*.	Ugliness; malice.
Maskililaidgua*wôgan*.	Pock-marks.
Matôlawzo*wôgan*.	Leanness, thinness.
Sôglamalso*wôgan*.	Health.

SICKNESS, DISEASE.

Akuamalso*wôgan*.	Illness; disease.
Madamalso*wôgan*	Indisposition.

---

1. In general, by suppressing the two syllables *wô-gan* from the substantives having that termination, as above, we have the indicat. pres. 3*d* pers. sing. of a verb; as thus: *msinasa*, he (she) sighs; *kôgôlwa*, he (she) crys; *akuamalso*, he (she) is sick.

Mdupinawôgan.		Headache.
Obidôgwôgan, *or* ôbidawas.		Toothache.
Wessagagzawôgan.		Stomach *or* belly ache.
Kezabzowôgan.		Fever.
Nônôgıpozowôgan.		Coldfits; shivering.
Wjibilwas.		A fit.
Wanôdaminwôgan.		Hydrophobia, madness.
Wesguinawôgan *or* wesgoinôgan.		A cold; a cough.
Taakui nasawôgan.		Short breath.

PARTS OF THE BODY.

Mhaga.[1]	5	The body.
Mdup.	5	The head.
Wdupkuanal.		The hair of the head.
Msizukw.	7	The face; eye.
Mdon; mejôl.		The mouth, the nose.
Wanowaal.		The cheeks; his, her—.
Mdôppikan.	5	Chin.
Wilalo.	5	The tongue, his, her—.
Wibidal.		The teeth, his, her—.
Wkuedôgan.	5	The neck; his, her—.
Mdolka.	5	The stomach.
Mlawogan.	5	The heart.
Mlagzi.	5	The belly.
Mlagzial.		The bowels.
Mdelmôgan.	1	The shoulder.
Wkeskouan.	5	The back; his, her—.
Môigan.	5	The loins, the reins.
Mzabi.	5	The hip.
Wpedin, *ta* wkôd.	5	The arm *and* the leg.
Melji *ta* mezid.	5	The hand *and* the foot.
Mkeskuan.	5	The elbow.
Mkedukw.	3	The knee.
Mkazak.		The nails.

1. Whenever the *adjective possessive* n. k, or w, is to be prefixed to a noun expressing any part of the body, commencing in *m;* as, *mhaga, mdup, mlawôgan,* this letter (m) must be suppressed before prefixing the possessive adjective; as thus: *nhaga,* my body; *kdup,* your head; *wlawôgan,* his (her) heart.

Wilidebôn *ta* win.		The brain *and* the marrow.
Pagakan.		The blood.
Wskan.	4	The bone.
Kôjoak.		The veins.
Wejat*al.*		The nerves.
Wizôwilahwôgan.		The jaundice.
Pzejilahwôgan.		A fainting-fit; a swoon.
Maskilhôgan.		The small-pox.
Pazisilhawôgan.		The measles.
Kiwanaskua Ihawôgan.		Giddiness.
Maguizowôgan.		A swelling.
Pmowa.		A boil.
Wagsozowôgan.		A cut (with a knife).
Wagtahozowôgan.		A cut (with an axe).
Majimalômilhawôgan.		Hooping cough.
Mannachôgowôgan.		Consumption.

WEARING APPAREL.

Wôhôbaks.	1	A shirt.
Nôpkowan.	5	The neck tie.
Ptenôgan*ak.*		The sleeves.
Aalômkôzik plejes.		Drawers.
Plejes.	5	A pair of breeches, trousers.
Lôbakhigan*al.*		Suspenders.
Medas*al.*		Socks.
Phanemi-medas*al.*		Stockings.
Kiganôbi*al.*		Garters.
Pots*al.*		Boots.
Mkezen*al.*		Shoes; moccasins.
Pitkôzon; silki—.	5	A coat; a silk gown.
Kchi pitkôzon.	5	An overcoat.
Silad.	5	A waistcoat; a vest.
Pidôgon*al.*		The pockets.
Patnes*al.*		The buttons.
Patnesôlagol.		The buttonholes.
Pitoguônsôgan.		The lining.
Piguônsôgan.		The trimming.

Nôbkoan.	7	The collar.
Kchi-patôn.	5	A cloak.
Kwutguabizon	5	A girdle; a belt.
Pilwôntukw.	5	A wig.
Asolkwôn.	5	A hat.
Moswa.	5	A handkerchief.
Aaliljômuk*ik*.		Gloves.
Naskuahon.	1	A comb.
Tbahïkisosôgan	5	A watch.
O'nkawahlagiadigan*al*.		The chain.
Pkwessagahigan	5	The key.
Sakhiljalion.	5	A ring (finger ring).
Nibawiljahon.	5	A wedding ring.
Chigitwahigan.	5	A razor.
Wsizugwaigan*al*.		Spectacles.
Nadialwalhakw.	7	A hunting-knife.
Tmokuataigan.	5	A sword.
O'badahon.	5	A cane; a walking-stick.
O'badahon.	5	A crutch.
Labizowan.	5	A petticoat.
Alômabizowan.	5	An under-petticoat.
Tablia.	5	An apron.
Phanemi-pitkôzon.	5	A gown.
Kchi-moswa.	5	A shawl.
Pipinawjakwôgan.	5	A looking glass.
Pinsis*ak*.		Pins.
Saksahon.	5	An earring.
Silki.	5	A ribbon.
Mizôwimôniinôkwkil.		Jewels.
Phanemasolkwôn.	5	A bonnet.
Mskikoasolkwôn.	5	A straw hat.
Wpedinôbial.		Bracelets.
O'basawwan.	1	A fan.
Liguônsôgan.	5	A thimble.
Kalizad.	5	Flannel.
Mômôlagen.	7	Calico.
Whawlatagak.	6	Fine cloth, woollen cloth.
Silki.	5	Silk, satin, ribbon.
Aazatak.	6	Crape.

OF THE TABLE, MEALS AND DISHES

Tawipodi.	5	A table.
Wlôganinôkwkil.		Table utensils; plate.
Papkuedanôzik.	6	A sideboard.
Tawipodiagen.	5	The tablecloth.
Kasiljawwan.	5	A towel.
Napkin.	5	A napkin.
Anasiat.	5	A plate; a cover.
Nsakuakw.	7	A knife.
Nimatguahigan.	5	A fork.
Amkuôn.	1	A spoon.
Kchi wlôgan.	5	A soup-tureen.
Kwatsis.	1	A cup.
Aazasit.	2	A glass.
Kchi aazasit.	2	A tumbler.
Potôiia.	1	A bottle.
Pinagel.		Vinegar.
Pinageli-kwatis.	1	The vinegar-cruet.
Pemi.		Oil; grease.
Pemii-kwatis.	1	The oil-cruet.
Siwan.		Salt.
Siwani-kwatis.		The salt-cellar.
Whawizôwjagak.		Mustard.
Whawizôwjagaki-kwatis.	1	The mustard-pot.
Tipwabel.		Pepper.
Tipwabelinodasis.		The pepper-box.
Agômnoki-moskuaswaskw.		Ginger.
Lamiskad. (fr. la muscade).		The nutmeg.
Sogal.		Sugar.
Sogali kwat.		The sugar-basin.
O'mwaimlases.		Honey.
Mlases.		Molasses.
Pkuazigan.		Bread.
Alipimek.		A meal.
Wspôsipowôgan.		Breakfast.
Kasilawabosowôgan.		The dessert; a lunch.
Paskuaipowôgan.		Dinner.
Adlôgwipowôgan.		Supper.

Ti.		Tea.
Kzôbo.		Broth; soup.
Nsôbôn.		Soup; corn-soup.
Lasob; pizilasob.		Soup; pea-soup.
Wôbi malomenisal.		Rice soup; rice.
Taliozigan.		Boiled meat.
Mkuejazigan.		Roast meat.
Lago.		A stew.
Segueskejakhigan.		A fricassee; a hash.
Kaoziia.		Beef.
Mkuejazigan kaoziia.		Roast beef.
Kaozisiia.		Veal.
Azibiia.		Mutton; lamb.
Azibi-wpigasinol.		Mutton-chops.
Azibigan.		A leg of mutton.
Wodolloak.		Kidneys.
Kalkia azibiia.		A quarter of lamb.
Piksiia		Pork; bacon.
Piksi-wpigasen.		A porkchop.
Wibalasigan.		Ham.
Podinak.		Black pudding
Nolkaiia.		Venison.
Awaasiia or awaaswiia.		Game.
Ahamoiia.		Poultry.
Wulguan.		A wing.
Namas; naimasila.		Fish; some fish.
Alsak.		Oysters.
Sôgak.		Lobsters.
Nahômoiak.		Eels.
Padatesak.		Potatoes.
Kabij.	5	A cabbage.
Wôwanal.		Eggs.
Taliodagil wôwanal.		Boiled eggs.
Wski-wôwanal or wskôwanal.		New laid eggs.
Pata.	4	A tart, a pie.
Abônak or abônisak.		Cakes.
Kalakonak.		Biscuits (sea biscuits).
Chiz.		Cheese.
Wisôwipemi.		Butter.

Minôbo.	Preserves, jam.
Pôngoksak.	Pancakes.

BEVERAGES.

Nebi.	Water.
Nbisonbi.	Mineral water.
Labial.	Beer; ale.
Labialsis.	Small beer.
Saidal.	Cider.
Makwbagak.	Wine.
Ngôni makwbagak.	Old wine.
Wski makwbagak.	New wine.
Wôbi makwbagak.	White wine.
Plachmônimakwbabak	French wine.
Akwbi.	Rum.
Weski.	Whiskey.
Jin.	Gin.
Blandi.	Brandy.
Kadosmoôganal.	Liquors.

FRUIT AND FRUIT TREES.

Aples.	1	An apple.
Aplesakuam.	1	An apple tree.
Azawanimen.	1	A plum.
Azawanimenakuam.	1	A plum tree.
Adbimen.	5	A cherry.
Adbimenakuam.	1	A cherry tree.
Wasawas.	5	An orange.
Môlôgowimenal.		Grapes.
Somenak.		Raisins.
Pagôn; pagônis.	5	A walnut; a hazlenut.
Sgueskimenak.		Raspberries.
Sgueskimenimozi.		A raspberry bush.
Mskikoiminsak.		Strawberries.
Psakwdamenak.		Mulberries.
Adotomenal.	1	Beam-tree berries.
Pessimenal.		Currants.

Wajoimen*al*.		Beech-nuts.
Sata.	8	Blueberry.
Satamozi.	5	Blueberry bush.
Piches*ak*.		Peaches.
Kôwakwimen.	1	A gooseberry.
Pagônis*al*.		Chestnuts; filberts.
Anaskemen.	5	An acorn.
Popokua.	8	A cranberry.

FOREST-TREES, FLOWERS, ETC.

Anaskemezi.	1	An oak.
Anibi.	1	An elm.
Wawabibagw.	3	A poplar.
Wajoimizi.	1	A beech.
Mahlakws.	1	An ash.
Senomozi.	1	A maple.
Maskwamozi.	1	A birch.
Wdopi.	5	An alder-tree.
Kokokhôakw.	3	A fir-tree.
Saskib.	5	An elder.
Kanozas.	1	A willow.
Môlôdagw.	3	A cedar.
Wigbimizi.	1	Bass wood.
Chignazakuam.	1	A thorn-tree.
Moskwaswaskw.	7	The sweet-flag.
Maskwazimenakuam.	1	A wild-cherry tree.
Nibimenakuam.	1	A bush-cranberry tree.
Alnisedi.	1	A hemlock.
Sagaskôdagw.	3	Ground-hemlock.
Pasaakw.	3	A red pine.
Msoakw.	3	A dry tree; decayed wood.
Temanakw.	7	A stub, *or* a broken tree.
Papagakanilhôk.		Bloodroot.
Ahadbak.		A vensroot.
Alnôbai tipoabel.		Wild ginger.
Chijis.	1	Wild onion.
Masozi*al*.		Ferns.
Skibô.	4	The ground-nut *or* indian potato.

Asakuam.		Moos.
Wanibagw.	7	A leaf.
Wlemskw.	7	A blossom.
Wajapk.	7	A root.
Kawasen.		A wind-fall.
Walagaskw.	3	Bark.
Maskwa.	8	Birch-bark.
Pskaôtkwen.	7	A branch.
Wskidakuam.		The sap.
Alômakuam.		The heart of a tree.
Awazonal.		Fuel, firewood.
Msazesso.	1	White spruce.
Mskak.	1	Black spruce.
Pôbnôdageso.	1	Tamarac.
Sasôgsek.		Sarsaparilla.

MECHANICAL ARTS, ETC.

Noji-kadôbidaphowad	2	A dentist.
Noji-paskhiganikat.	2	A gun-smith.
Noji-tbakwnigad.	2	A land surveyor.
Noji-chigetowawwat.	2	A barber.
Noji-aseswôbikad.	2	A harness-maker.
Nodbaadigat.	2	A washer-woman.
Nodkwahid.	2	A woodman, wood cutter.
Nodabônkad.	2	A baker.
Môni nojinademiwad.	2	A banker; a broker.
Nodônkolhôd.	2	A merchant.
Noji-pakhiminad	2	A thresher.
Noji-mônikad.	2	A jeweller.
Nodasolkwônkat.	2	A hatter.
Nojikkad.	2	A carpenter; joiner.
Nodôjiphowad.	2	A carter; carman.
Nojiguônsad.	2	A seamster; tailor.
Nojiguônsaskua.	4	A seamster.
Nodagisôwad.	2	A tailor.
Nobatebit.	2	A cook.
Notkezenikad.	2	A shoemaker.
Klosli.	1	A grocer.

Nodalhagokad.	2	A blacksmith.
Noji-papawijokad.	2	A tinsmith.
Noji-pskwasawônkad	2	A florist.
Noji-tbaikisosôganikad	2	A watchmaker.
Mahôwad.	2	A landlord.
Mahôwadiskwa.	4	A landlady.
Soghebat.	2	An inn-keeper; hotel-keeper.
Noji-alnalhakwawighigad.	2	A printer.
Notkazôwad.	2	A plough-man.
Noji-kawakwnigad.	2	A reaper.
Nodapskenigad.	2	A mason.
Nodapskaigad	2	A stone-cutter.
Nottahasid.	2	A miller.
Noji-nbizonhowad.	2	A physician, a doctor.
Nadazoonigad.	2	A horse-dealer.
Noji-wizôwimônikad.	2	A goldsmith.
Nodômad.	2	A fisherman.
Noji-sezowigad.	2	A painter.
Nodatsigad.	2	A tanner, a dyer,
Noji-abaznodakad.	2	A basketmaker.
Noji-tbelodmowinno.	1	An advocate, a barrister
Nodawighigad.	2	A notary public.
Noji-sôglitigad.	2	A registrar.
Noji-môniad.	2	A treasurer.
Nodôbaktahigad.	2	A fidler.
Noji-pakholid.	2	A drummer,
Notkikad.	2	A sower; a tiller.
Nadialwinno.	1	A hunter.
Notkuaag.	2	A pilot.

OF THE SEA.

Sobagw.	7	The ocean; the sea.
Mani menahanikak.	6	An archipelago; at the.
Menahan.	7	An island.
Menahanakamigw.	7	A peninsula.
Senodkamigwa, senojiwi.	6	The shore.
Pamkaak.		The coast.
Wisawôgamak.	6	A strait.

Tegoak.		The waves.
Awiben.		A calm; it is——.
Pitah.		The foam; the froth.
Pamapskak.	6	A rock.
Mamilahômak.	6	A promontory.
O'dawômkak.	6	A sand bank.
Kzelômsen.		The wind;——blows.
Petguelômsen.		A whirlwind.
Kokw.	1	A whirlpool.

DOMESTIC ANIMALS, WILD QUADRUPEDS, BIRDS, FURS AND SKINS

Ases, aaso.	1	A horse.
N'-d-aasom,	1	My horse.
Kaoz; (——awa).	1	A cow; (a——hide).
Wski asesis.	1	A colt; a filly.
Aksen.	1	An ox.
Kaozis.	1	A calf; a heifer.
Sponioli ases.	1	A mule; an ass.
Azib; (——awa)	1	A sheep; (a.——skin).
Azibis.	1	A lamb.
Kots; kotsis.	1	A goat; a kid.
Minowis, pezois.	1	A cat.
Alemos, adia.	1	A dog.
Wski alemos.	1	A young dog.
(N-d-amis,	1	My dog.
Piges, piks; *piksak*		A pig; pigs.
Pitôlo.	1	A lion.
Môlsem; (—is).	3	A wolf; (a young—).
Wôkwses.	1	A fox.
Pakesso.	1	A partridge.
Mateguas.	1	A hare; a rabbit.
Mikowa.	1	A squirrel.
Wôbikwsos.	1	A mouse.
Tmakwa; (—awa).	4	A beaver; (—skin)
(Tmakwaiia,		Beaver meat).
Moskuas; (—wawa).		A muskrat; (—skin).
Wnegigw.	1	An otter.

Wlanigw; (—sis).	1	A fisher; (a young—).
Mosbas.	1	A mink.
Apanakes.	1	A marten, sable.
Psanigw.	1	A black squirrel.
Planigw.	1	A flying squirrel.
Moz; (—agen;—ia).	1	Moose; (——skin;—meat).
Magôlibo; (—awa).	1	A carribou; (a—skin).
Nolka; (—iia).	4	A deer; (venison).
Kôgw; (—is).	1	A porcupine. (a young—).
Saguasis.	1	A weasel.
Akigw; (—awa).	1	A seal (a—skin).
Akigwawaiia.		Of seal-skin.
Segôgw.	1	A skunk.
Awasos.	1	A bear.
Pziko; (—makwsessis).		A buffalo; (a yearling—).
Pziko aioba. (pl.—ak—k).		A female buffalo, a bull.
Pziko allha.* (pl.—ak—k).		A female buffalo.
Pziko kadnadokw.	1	A two year old buffalo.
Wdosoallha peziko.		A three year old buffalo.
Anikwses.	1	A "striped squirrel."
Asban.	1	A racoon.
Agaskw.	3	A woodchuck.
Sips; sibsis.	1	A bird; a little bird.
Sips nôbalha † (pl.—ak—k).		A male bird.
Sips skualha † (pl.—ak—k).		A female bird.
Mgeso; mgesois.	1	An eagle; an eaglet.
Kokokhas; walôias.	1	An owl.
O'basas.	1	A woodpecker.
Kwiguigum.	3	A black duck.
Mama.	4	A black woodpecker.
Madagenilhas.		A bat.
Wisôwihlasis.	1	A wizard, (or any other kind of yellow bird).
Cheskwadadas.	1	A king-fisher.
Sasaso.	1	A plover.
Siômo.		A bird of prey.

---

* Spell: *al-tha*;
† Spell: *nô-ba-lha; skua-lha*

Sasasois, (*pron*:—wis).	1	A small species of plover.
Kwikueskas.	1	A robin.
Kejegigilhasis, (*spell*:—Ihasis).		A chickadee.
Chimeliilhasis.	1	A chimney swallow.
Mkazas; kchimkazas.	1	A crow; raven.
Kaskaljas *or* Kaskaljasis.	1	A song-sparrow.
Kaakw; Kaakwis.	3, 1	A gull; a small grey gull.
Wlôgowilhas.		A nightingale.
Pokui sigoskuasis.		The wheat-ear.
Ahamo; ahamois.	1	A hen; chicken.
Nôbalha.	4	A cock; a male bird.
Wôbigilhakw.	3	A goose.
Nahama.	4	A turkey.
Pôlôbai-sibes, (plur.—sipsak).		A peacock.
Mdawilha;—sis.	4,1	A loon; a young—.
Alônteguilha, (spell:—lha).	4	A wood duck.
Nanatasis.	1	A humming bird.
Sobagwilha.	4	A sea duck.
Nbesi-chogleskw.	3	A bobolink.
Chogleskw.	3	A cow-bunting.
Pnegôkihlasis.	1	A bank swallow.
Tidesso.	1	A blue jay.
Wôbtegua.	4	A wild-goose.
Pelaz.	1	A wild pigeon.
Wôbipelaz.	1	A pigeon, (tame—).
Pakesso.	1	A partridge.
Seguanilha,* (spell:—lha).	4	A smiter-hawk.*
Soglonilhasis.	1	A swallow.
Wigualha.	4	A swan.
Pokhamenes.		A bittern.
Kasko.		A heron.
Alômsaguilhasis.		A whin chat.
Papoles.		A whip-poor-will.

* A bird that kills its prey with a blow with its breast bone.

FISHES, REPTILES AND INSECTS

Namas.	1	A fish.
Kabasa.	4	A sturgeon.
Nokamagw.	3	A cod.
Makelo.	1	A mackerel.
Tolba.	4	A turtle.
Sôga.	4	A lobster.
Als*ak*.		Oysters; shells.
Mskuamagw.	3	A salmon.
Kwenoza.	4	A pike.
Wôbhagas.	1	A carp.
Kikômkwa.	4	A sucker.
Namagw.	3	A salmon trout.
Nahômo.	1	An eel.
Wôbi namas *or* wôbamagw.	1	A white fish.
Watagua.	4	A pickerel.
Môlazigan.	1	A bass.
Skog.	1	A serpent; a snake.
Chegual.	1	A frog,
Maska *or* mamaska.	4	A toad.
Kakadôlôgw.	1	A lizard.
Pabaskw.	3	A leech, a bloodsucker.
Msaskog.	1	A Boa.
Skoks.	1	A worm.
Sisikwa.	4	A rattle snake.
Mamselabika.	4	A spider.
Sigiliamo.	1	A locust.
Chôls.	4	A cricket.
Maskejamôgwses.	1	A bug.
Pabigw.	1	A flea.
Alikws.	1	An ant, a pismire.
Kemô.	4	A louse.
Mamijôla.	4	A butterfly.
Wawilômwa.	4	A bee; a wasp
Kchi wawilômwa.		A drone.
Wjawas.	1	A fly.
Massakua.	4	A horsefly.
Pegues.	1	A mosquito.

OF THE COUNTRY AND THE OBJECTS MET WITH.

Odana.	5	A town; a city; a village.
O'wdi.		A road; a street.
O'wdesis.	5	A path.
Ki; aki.	5	An estate; a farm; land.
Wigwôm, (gamigw)		A house.
Negôni gamigw.		An old house.
Kinjamesigamigw.	7	A castle; a palace.
Aiamihawigamigw.	7	A church
Taguahôgan.	5	A mill.
Pessakuôgan.	5	A saw-mill.
Kaozigamigw.	7	A stable.
Kchikaozigamigw.	7	A barn.
Soghebaigamigw.	7	An inn, a tavern.
Psakaigan.	6	A ditch.
Pmelodigan.	5	A fence.
Pmelodiganakuam*al*.		Fence rails.
Skahôgan*ak*.		Pickets.
Sibo, tegw, ttegw.	1	A river.
Sibos; sibosis.	5	A brook; a little brook.
Kpiwi.		A forest; in the—.
Pami pizagak.		The bush; in the—.
Nbizonkikôn.	5	A garden.
Kikôn.	5	A field.
Maji ki *or* mamadaki	5	A barren land; poor—.
Wli ki.	5	A fertile land.
Kawakwnigawôgan.		The harvest.
Mskagw.		A marsh.
Tebeskahigan.	5	A hay-stack.
Nodahlagokaigamigw	7	A forge.
Azib*ak*.		A flock of sheep; sheep.
Nidazo*ak*.		A herd of cattle; cattle; animals.
Kanal.	5	A canal.
Alnahlagwôwdi.	5	A railway.
Lessaguôgan.	5	A bridge.
Notchôguaigamigw.	7	An hospital.
Kbahodwigamigw.	7	A prison, a jail.

Kaas.	A car.
Kdakinna.	The globe.

MONEY AND COINS.

Môni.	Money; silver.
Sakwskigek.	Change.
Pilaskwi-môni.	A bank-note.
Wizôwi-môni.	Gold; a gold coin.
Somalkin.	Halfpenny.
Sans.	One cent.
Mdalasis.	A dime (10 cts).
Mdala sansak.	Ten cents.
Pinso.	A franc (10 pence).
Silôn.	A shilling (20 cts).
Tlôtso, *or* nisinska taba nôlan sansak.	Twenty-five cents.
Pazeko môni.	One dollar.
Pazeko lowi.	A pound.

WEIGHTS AND MEASURES.

Mdala lowiak.	Ten pounds (£10).
Ngueji tkwiguan.	A pound.
Pabasi tkwiguan.	Half a pound.
Kaltlo.	Quarter of a pound.
Awens.	An ounce.
Minot.	A bushel (8 gallons).
Temiminot.	Half a bushel.
Minot taba pabasiwi.	A bushel and half.
Nguet'galanoo.	A gallon.
Mdala Kas'galanoo.	Ten gallons.
Pabas'galanoo.	Half a gallon.
Nguet'kwatoo.	A quart (a quarter of a gallon).
Pabasba.	A pint.
Nguet'akwnôso *or* pazegueda llakwnôso.	One yard.
Pabasi llakwnôso.	Half a yard.
Nguejipia taba pabasiwi.	A foot and a half.

Nguet' ak wiadôgan.		An inch.
Mail. (*pron*: ma-il).		A mile.
Nguet'osômguat.		A league.
Nguet'osômguat tmeskuiwi.		A square league.
Alpôn ki.		An acre of land.

CORN AND VEGETABLES.

Malomen*al*.		Wheat.
Asesowimen*al*.		Oats.
Nagakowimen*al*.		Rye.
Tlots*al*.		Barley.
Skamon*al*.		Indian corn.
Wajabk*al*.		Roots.
Mskiko*al*.		Hay.
Mskikois*al*.		Herbs.
Atebakwa*al or* tebaku*al*.		Beans.
Channaps*ak*.		Turnips.
Kabij.	5	A cabbage.
Timeno.	5	A melon.
Askitameg.	6	A cucumber.
Winos.	1	An onion.
Winosis*ak*.		Shallots.

FARMING IMPLEMENTS, CARRIAGES, HARNESS, ETC, ETC.

Lakazôwôgan.	5	A plough.
Lakazôwawôgan.		Ploughing, act of—.
Nokapodigan.	5	A harrow.
N'-d-elkazôwôgan.		My plough.
N'nokapodigan.		My harrow.
Nokapodigawôgan.		Harrowing, act of—.
N'nokapodiga.		I harrow.
N'-d-elkazôwa.		I plough.
Lakaigan.	5	A hoe.
Temaskezôwôgan.		Scythe.
N'temskezôwôgan.		My scythe.
N'temskezôwa.		I mow.
Temaskezôwa.		He mows.

Wôlkogan.	5	A shovel.
Magôlhigan.	1	A wooden shovel.
Mskikoi - nimateguaigan.	5	A hay-fork.
Aalôbidaak.	5	A rake.
Wagin.	1	A waggon.
Wakôlikws.	6	A wheel; a cart.
Aseswôbial.		A harness.
Pihanisak.		The reins.
Nobalobi.		A bridle.
Sazamhigan.		A whip.
Tawabodi.		A saddle.
Wawabigôdhigan.		A sleigh.

COLOURS, PAINTING, WRITING IMPLEMENTS, ETC.

Mkui... (in the composition).		Red.
Mkuigen.	pl. *ol*	It is red.
Mkuigo.	" *ak*	He, she, it, is red.
Mkui sezowigan.		Red paint.
Sezowigan.	" *al*	Paint.
Mkui sezowôzo.		He, she, it, is painted red
Atsigan.	" *al*	Dye.
Mku'atsigan.		Red dye.
N'-d-atsiga.		I dye.
N'moku'atsiga.		I dye red.
N'-d-atsô.		I dye him, her, (it).
N'-d-atsemen.		I dye it.
N'-d-atsemenana.		We dye it.
K'-d-atsemenana.		We dye it.
Wlôwi...		Blue.
Wlôw'atsigan.		Blue dye.
Wlôwigo.		He, she, it, is blue.
Wlôwigen.		It is blue.
Wlôwi sezowigan.		Blue paint.
Mkuôbamegua.		Reddish.
Wlôwôbamegua.		Bluish.
Wizôwi...		Yellow.
Wizôwi kezabezowôgan.		Yellow fever.

Wizôw'atsigan.		Yellow dye.
Wizôwigen.		It is yellow.
Askaskui...		Green.
Askaskui sezowigan.		Green paint.
Askasku' atsigan.		Green dye.
W-d-askaku'atsemen.		He, she, dyes it green
Wôbi...		White.
Wôbigen.		It is white.
Wôbigo.		He, she, it, is white.
Wôbi gamigw.	7	A white house.
Wôbipegw.		Lime.
Mkazawi...		Black.
Mkazawigen.		It is black.
Mkazawigo.		He, she, it, is black;
Wôbigek.		The white.
Makazawigek.		The black.
Wôbbagak.		The white, (liquid).
Makazawbagak.		The black, (liquid).
Wôbbaga.		It is white, (liquid).
Mkazawbaga.		It is black, (liquid).
Awighiganebi.		Some ink.
N'-d-awighiganebim wlôwbaga.		My ink is blue.
N'pilaskom wôbigen.		My paper is white.
N'miguenom wôbigo.		My pen is white.
Miguen.	3	A pen, a quill; a feather
Wdamdôôobamegua.		It is brown.
Minôbowigen.		It is violet.
Minôbowigek.		The violet.
Wibgui...		Grey; drab.
Wibguigen.		It is grey.
Wibguigo.		He, she, it, is grey.
W'-d-asolkwôn wibeguigen.		His (her) hat is grey.
Wibguigek asolkwôn.[1]		A or the grey hat.
Wibguigo n'-d-aasom.		My horse is grey.
Wibguigoa w'-d-asoma.		His (her) horse is grey.
Sen or asen.		A slate; a stone.

---

1. We say also: *wibgu'asolkwôn.*

CARDINAL POINTS, etc.

Sôwanaki ⎫ Ali-paskuat ⎬ Nibenaki ⎭	The South.
Sowanakik ⎫ Nibenakik ⎬ Ali-paskuat ⎭	Southward, at, to, from the South.
Sowanessen.	South wind, the wind comes from the South.
Pebonki.	The North.
Pebonkik.	Northward at, to, from the North.
Pebonkiak.	Northern people.
Waji-nahilôt ⎫ Waji-sôkhipozit ⎬	The East; at, to, from the East.
Sobhôban.	Day break.
Kirzôban.	It is day light.
Kizôbak.	At day light.
Wôbanaki *or* O'banaki.	Land of the East.
Wôbanakiak. (*singular,* Wôbanaki).	The people (Indians) from where the sun rises.
Ali-nkihlôt.	The West, westward; at, to, from the west.
Ali-nkihlôt weji pmôwzowinnoak.	The western people.
Nibenakiak, (*singular,* nibenaki).	The southern people.
Nsawiwi ali-paskuat ta ali-nkihlôt.	South-west; at, to, from the south-west.
Nsawiwi pebonkik ta waji-nahilôt.	North-East; at, to, from the north-east.
Nsawiwi waji-nahilôt ta ali-paskuat.	South-east; at, to, from the south-east.
Nsawiwi pebonkik ta aji-nkihlôt.	North-west; at, to, from the north-west.

HUNTING AND FISHING IMPLEMENTS, ETC.

Paskhigan.	5	A gun.
Adebôlagw.	7	A rifle.
Nahnisakwtag.	6	A double-barreled gun.

Abenaki		English
Papkwesbalôg paskigan.		A breech-loader.
Papkweskalôg*il* paskhigan*al*.		Breech-loaders.
Alômsawaiias.	5	A pistol; a revolver.
Saguôlhigan.	5	A ramrod.
Asenapanes.	1	The lock.
Alemos.	1	The cock; the hammer.
Tôbi.	1	A spring; a bow.
Nhanesnôsik.	6	The trigger.
Peza.		The powder.
Sasalhôgil (sissalhogil).		Shot.
Mamsag.	6	A ball, a bullet.
Telaps.	1	A steel-trap.
Klahigan.	5	A wooden-trap.
N'telapsem.	1	My steel-trap.
N'kelhigan.		My wooden-trap.
Kap *or* Kapsis.	5	A percussion-cap, a cap.
Pidapskuiganinoda.	5	The shot-belt.
Askan.	1	A powder-horn; a horn.
Nadialowinno.	1	A hunter; a sportsman.
Nadialoi ki.		Hunting ground.
Pisowakamigw.	7	The wilderness.
Pisowakamigwinno.	1	An uncivilized man or person.
Nadialowôgan.		Hunting.
O'mawôgan.		Fishing.
Chawapenigan *or* chawpenigan.		A fish hook.
Chawapeniganatagw.	7	A fishing line.
Chawapeniganakuam.	5	A fishing rod.
Nodamaguôngan.	1	A fishspear.
Awôgan.		The bait.
Lhab *or* ahlab.	1	A net.
N-d-ahlabem,—ak.		My net—nets.
K'-d-ahlabem.		Your (thy) net.
W'-d-ahlbema.		His (her) net, *or* nets.
N'-dahlabomna;—wak		Our net—nets.
K'-d-ahlabemna.		Our net.
W'-d-ahlabemowô.		Their net, *or* nets.

ECCLESIASTICAL AND SECULAR DIGNITIES.

Kchi Sôgmôwi - Patlihôz.	1	The Pope, the Sovereign Pontiff.
Sôgmowi patlihôz.	1	A Bishop.
Kchi patlihôz.	1	A parish priest, a high-priest.
Patliliôz.	1	A priest.
Manistel.	1	A minister.
Kinômasowinno.	1	A preacher.
Patlihôskua.	4	A nun.
Kinjames.	1	A king.
Kinjamesiskua.	4	A queen.
Kinjamessis.	1	A prince.
Kinjamessiskuasis.	1	A princess.
Saniol;—iskua.		A lord; a lady.
Kchisôgmôi lidebezwinno.		A minister of state.
Kchi sôgmô;—skua.		A governor; the-'s wife.
Sôgmô;—skua.		A chief; chief's wife.
Kaptin.	1	A captain.
Kolnal.	1	A colonel.
Pastoni-Kchi Sôgmo.		The President of the U.S. of America.

GAMES, RECREATIONS, etc.

Pemegawôgan,		Dancing.
N'pemegô.		I dance.
Pemega.		He (she) dances.
Pemegawinno.	1	A dancer.
Alôgmapozimuk.		To skate.
K'-d-alogmapozi.		Thou art skating.
Lôgmapoza.		He (she) is skating.
Lôgmapozowinno.	1	A skater.
Lôgmapozowan*ak*.		Skates.
Telap*ak*,		Cards.
Negueji chebezoak tela*pak*.		A pack of cards.
Naguedawighôsit.	2	The ace.
Sôgmô.	4	The king.
Awanochwi-skuaso.	1	The queen.
Wsemôganes.	1	The knave.

Nises or nis.	1	The deuce.
Awskatastigamuk.		To shuffle.
Nadonômuk.		To cut.
N'nadonô.		I cut.
Nadona.		He (she) cuts.
Agisowanak.		Counters.
Pabaskwhamawôgan.		Playing-ball or play-ball
Pabaskhamôgan.	1	A ball.
N'telaphamô.		I play at card.
N'pabaskwhamô.		I play at ball.
Pabaskwhama.		He (she) plays at ball.
Pabasbwhamak.		They play at ball.
Lôbaktaigan; tôbi.	5	A fiddle; a bow.
Piguôngan.	5	A flute; a fife.
Pakholigan.	1	A drum.
Kchi-lôbaktaigan.	5	A piano; an organ.
Lintowôgan.	5	A song.

NAMES OF CITIES, TOWNS, VILLAGES, RIVERS, COUNTRIES, NATIONS, ETC., ETC.

Molian.	Montreal.
Moliani.	A Montrealer.
Moliniak.	Montrealers.
Moliantegw.	River St-Lawrence.
Masessolian.	Sorel.
Masessolianiak.	Sorellers.
Masessoliantegw.	River Chambly.
Madôbalodnik.	Three-Rivers.
Madôbalodniak.	People or inhabitants of Three-Rivers.
Madôbalodnitegw.	River St-Maurice.
Palkinek.	Berthier.
Palkiniak.	Peop. or inhabitants of Berthier.
Pithiganek.	Nicolet.
Pithiganiak.	Peop. or inhabitants of Nicolet.
Pithiganitegw.	River Nicolet.
Wôlinak.	Becancour.
Welinaktegw.	River Becancour.

Padiskônek.	Batiscan.
O'bamasek.	Rivière du Loup (en bas).
O'bamasisek.	Yamachiche.
Pamadenainak.	Lorette (Ind. Village).
Pamadenai*ak*.	Indians of Lorette.
Kebek,[1] Kubek.[2] }	Quebec.
Kubeki.	A citizen (man) of Quebec.
Kuibekiak.	Peop. or inhabitants of Quebec.
Kuibekiskua.	A lady (woman) from Quebec.
Kuibekiskuak.	Ladies of Quebec.
Kaanawagi.	Caughnawaga.
Magua.	An Iroquois (indian).
Kaanawagihnono.	The iroquois tribe.
Otawa.	Ottawa.
Otawai.	A man (citizen) from Ottawa.
Otawaiiak.	People or inhabitants of Ottawa.
Koattegw.	Pine River.
Koattegok.	Coaticook.
Mamlawbagak.	Mamphremagog.
Môdôwa.	Mantawa.
Paliten.	Burlington.
Sôn-Halônek.	Plattsburg.
Salatogi.	Saratoga.
Nebizonbik.	At the mineral spring.
Kwenitegw.	River Connecticut.
Winoski.	Winooski.
Pasômsik.	Passumpsic.
Pamijoasik.	Pamigewasset.
Wiwninbesaki.	Winnipisaukee.
Wawôbadenik.	White mountain reg.
Wigwômadensisek.	St Hyacinthe.
Wigwômadenik.	Yamaska.
Kwanahômoik.	Durham.
Namakôttik.	Megantic.
Panaôbskak.	Penobscot.

---

1. Pronounce "Ke-bek" as in French, *Quebec.*
2. This *orthography* is an *imitation* of the English pronounciation.

Panaôbskattegw *or* Panaôbskai sibo.	Penobscot river.
Panaôbskaiiak.	People (indians) of Penobscot.
Kanada.	Canada.
Pastonki.	United States of America.
Pastonkik.	In the United States of America.
Pastoni.	An American.
Pastoniskua.	An American woman.
Iglismônki.	England.
Iglismônkik.	In England.
Iglismôn.	An Englishman.
Iglesmôniskua.	An English woman.
Plachmônki.	France.
Plachmôn.	A Frenchman.
Alemônki.	Germany.
Alemôn.	A German.
Spôniolki.	Spain.
Spôniol.	A Spaniard.
Illôdaki. (*pron.*–ak–ki).	Ireland.
Illôda.	An Irishman.
Illôdaskua.	An Irish woman.
Koswaki. (*pron.*–ak–ki).	Scotland.
Koswa.	A Scotchman.
Agômeneki.—(*pron* ak.—ki).	Europe.
Wdagômenoki. (*pl.*–ak).	An European.
Alsigôntegw. (*local term:* Alsigôntegok).	River St. Francis.
Alnôba.	An Indian.
Alnôbai phanem.	An Indian woman.
Wôbanaki.	An Abenaki (indian).
Sigwnigan.	A reserve.
Alnôbai sigwnigan.	An indian reserve.
Alnôbai lowôzowôgan *or* Alnôbawôzowôgan.	Indian costume.
Alnôba'odana.	An Indian village.
Plachmôni odana.	A French village.
Odana.	A city; town; village.
Ki, aki.	Earth, the globe, the world; country; farm; ground; soil.

N'-d-aki, w'-d-aki.	My farm, his (her) farm.
Kdakinna.	The globe. (*literally,* our earth, our globe).
K'-d-akinna.	Our farm *or* ground.

NAMES OF PERSONS WHICH DIFFER FROM BOTH, THE ENGLISH AND FRENCH ORTHOGRAPHY.

Sozap.	Joseph.
Pial.	Peter.
Tanial,	Daniel.
Azô.	John.
Ogistin.	Augustus.
Nikola.	Nicholas.
Tabid.	David.
Plasoa.	Francis.
Atian.	Stephen.
Sazal.	Cæsar.
Lazal.	Elijah.
Tomô.	Thomas.
O'bloas.	Ambrose.
Atoan.	Anthony.
Paslid.	Basil.
Pelnal.	Bernard.
Edoal.	Edward.
Klegual.	Gregory.
Islal.	Israel.
Salom.	Jerome.
Missal.	Michael.
Lobal.	Robert.
Simo.	Simon.
Lolô.	Lawrence.
Agat.	Agatha.
O'zalik.	Angelica.
O'nis.	Anna.
Sallot.	Charlotte.
Klistin.	Christiana.
O'nias.	Agnes.
Mali.	Mary.

Klalis.	Clarissa.
Amelain.	Emeline.
Alizôbat.	Elizabeth.
Alan.	Ellen.
Lowiz.	Louisa.
Sopi.	Sophia.
Toloti.	Dorothy.
Sessil.	Cicely.
Katetin.	Catherine.
Sozôn.	Susan.
Malgelit.	Margaret.
Talaz.	Theresa.

HOLIDAYS AND FESTIVALS.

Alamikôwadimuk.	New-year's day.
Kinjamesak.	Epiphany-Twelfth day
Wasanmômuk.	Candlemas.
Peguihodin.	Ash-Wednesday.
Sogmôwi Mali Kuasihômuk.	Lady day.
Sediak kalnômuk.	Palm Sunday.
O'bijibad.	Easter Sunday.
Spemkik alihlôd.	Ascension day.
Pamosaiamihômuk.	Corpus Christi day.
Skweda paskhôzik.	St. John-Baptist—Midsummer day.
Pialak Kuasihômuk.	St. Peter and St. Paul.
Sôgmôwi Missal Kuasihômuk,	Michaelmas day.
Pôbatamawawdimuk.	All Saints.
Nibôiamihômuk.	Christmas.
Môwsedowadoi kisokw	Dominion day.
Tebalmezoi kisokw.	Independence day.
Kinjamesiskua w'kiskom.	Queen's birth-day, (*lit.* Queen's day).
O'tkagôbadasi kisokw.	Arbour day.

SUBSTANTIVES HAVING NO SINGULAR.

Abasandôganal.	Aurore borealis, Northern lights.
Aiamihôganal.	Beads, chaplet.

O'nkawalagiadiganal.	A chain.
Aseswôbial.	A harness.
Pihanisak.	Reins.
Senômkol *or* senômkuisal.	Gravel.

As the Abenakis language has certain peculiarities which are not to be found in the English respecting the *plural* in *pronouns*, and that the use of those pronouns is to occur very often in the Second Part of this book, for the right distinction of their signification, I thought it convenient to give that *part of speech* before I close the First Part, notwithstanding that this be not the ordinary sequel of a Vocabulary. The next pages will therefore show you that part.

THE PERSONAL PRONOUNS.

1. Nominative Form.

Singular.	*Plural.*
1 *K,*' I.	1 *N,*'[1], we, (*exclusive*).
	1 *K,*'[2], we; (*inclusive*).
2 *K,*' thou	2 *K,*' you;
3 *W,*' he, she.	3 *W,*' they.

2. Objective Form.

Singular.	*Plural.*
1 *Nia,* me, (I;)	1 *Niuna,* us, to us, (we;)
	1 *Kiuna,* us, to us, (we;)
2 *Kia,* thee, (thou;)	2 *Kiuwô,* you, to you.
3 *Agma,* him, her, (she;)	3 *Agmôwô,* them, to them, (they).

---

1. Mind this well. *N,*' *niuna,* or *niunalla,* is employed, when those that speak *do not* include in their number the person or persons to whom they speak: *n'milsibena,* we eat, (we that speak, not the person or persons whom we speak to).

2. *K*' is used, when those that speak *include* in their number the person or persons to whom they speak: *K' pazôbibena,* we see, (we that speak, and the person or persons to whom we speak). And likewise *Kiuna, Kiunalla,* us, we, ourselves, that is, we altogether, those that speak, and those that are spoken to.

3. Reflective Form.

Singular.	Plural.
1 *Niatta*, myself;	1 *Niunalla*, ourselves, to—; (excl).
	1 *Kiunalla*, ourselves, to—; (incl).
2 *Kialla*, thyself;	2 *Kiuwôtla*, yourselves, to—;
3 *Agmatta*, himself, herself;	3 *Agmôwôtta*, themselves, to—;

THE POSSESSIVE PRONOUNS.

Singular.	Plural.
1 *Nia*, mine;	1 *Niuna*, ours, (excl).
	1 *Kiuna*, ours, (incl)
2 *Kia*, thine;	2 *Kiuwô*, yours;
3 *Agma*, his, hers;	3 *Agmôwô*, theirs.

N.–B.—Mind also that the *possessive adjectives n', k',* our, undergo the same peculiarities as the pronouns.

PART SECOND

The Elements
of
Abenakis Conversation.

VOCABULARY

Miguen.	A pen.
Awighiganebi.	Some ink.
Pilaskw.	Some paper.
Awighigan*al*.[1]	Some books.
Wissiguakhigan*al*.	Some envelopes.
Telaps.	A trap.
Paskhigan.	A gun.
Peza.	Some powder.
Sasahlôg*il*.	Some shot.
Wiguaol.	A bark-canœ.
O'gemak.	Snow shoes.
Wôôbaksigamigw.	A tent.
Tôbi.	A bow.
Pakua*al*.	Some arrows.
Abaznoda*al*.	Some baskets.
Aples*ak*.	Some apples.
Azawanimen*ak*.	Some plums.
Nibimen*al*	Some bush-cranberries.
Popoku*al*.	Some cranberries.
Adebimen*al*.	Some cherries.

USE OF THE VERB

Wajônômuk, wajônôzik, to have, with the foregoing nouns,
in the affirmative form.

N'wajônô miguen.	I have a pen.
'Wajônem awighiganebi.	He (she) has some ink.
N'wajônemebena pilaskw	We have some paper.
K'wajônemeba awighiganal.	You have some books.

---

1. The final *italics* mark the plural.

'Wajônemok wissiguakhiganal.	They have some envelopes,
N'wajônôb telaps.	I had a trap.
'Wajônemob paskhigan.	He (she) had a gun.
N'wajônemebenob peza	We had some powder.
K'wajônebôb sasahlôgil.	You had some shot.
'Wajônemobanik wiguaol.	They had a bark-canoe.
N'wajônôji ôgemak.	I shall have snow shoes
'Wajônemji wôôbaksigamigw.	He (she) will have a tent.
N'wajônôbenaji tôbi.	We shall have a bow.
K'wajônemebaji pakuaal.	You will have some arrows.
'Wajônemokji abaznodaal.	They will have some baskets.
N'wajônôba aplesak.	I should have some apples.
'Wajônaba azawanimena.	He (she) would have some plums.
N'wajônemebenaba nibimenal.	We should have some bush-cranberries.
K'wajônemebaba popokual.	You would have some cranberries.
'Wajônemokba adebimenal.	They would have some cherries.

VOCABULARY.

Mijowôgan.	Provisions.
Nokhigan.	Flour.
Moziia.	Moose-meat.
Pkuazigan.	Bread.
Wdamô.	Tobacco.
Wdamôgan.	Pipe.
Mkezenal.	Shoes, moccasins.
Temahigan.	An axe.
Alni-temahigan.	A tomahawk.
Lôbakhiganal.	Suspenders.
O'dolibiôgan.	An oar.
Temespanahon.	Scissors.
Lessagahigan.	A trunk.
Paks.	A box; chest.
Pkwessagahigan *or* pkwessaghigan.	A key.
Chigitwahigan.	A rasor.
Alokawôgan.	Work, labour.
Tebôbakhigan.	Scales; balance.

| Silkial. | Ribbons. |
| Aguanagiadïganal. | Curtains. |

USE OF THE VERB

Wajônômuk, wajônôzik, to have, with the foregoing nouns, in the negative form.

O'da n'wajônemow mijowôgan.	I have no provisions.
O'da wajônemowi nokhigan.	He (she) has no flour.
O'da n'wajônemoppena moziia.	We have no moose-meat.
O'da k'wajônôppa pkuazigan.	You have no bread.
O'da wajônawiak wdamô.	They have no tobacco.
O'da n'wajônôp wdamôgan.	I had no pipe.
O'da wajônemowip mkezenal.	He (she) had no shoes.
O'da n'wajônemoppenob temahigan.	We had no axe.
O'da k'wajônemoppôb alnitemahigan.	You had no tomahawk.
O'da 'wajônemowibanik lôbakhiganal.	They had no suspenders.

VOCABULARY OF ADJECTIVES.

(Simple and Invariable).

Wli.	Good; gentle.
Maji.	Bad, mean.
Kehi.	Great, big.
Msi, mamsi.	Large; vast.
Wski.	New; young.
Negôni, nôuegôni.	Old; ancient.
Wawasi.	Holy; sacred.
Sôgmôwi.	Saint.
Pili, pildowi.	New.
Wôbi.	White.
Mkazawi.	Black.
Sôgli.	Solid; stout.
Mliki.	Strong.

Noki.	Soft.
Pôgui.	Pure; genuine.
Sasagi.	Just; right.
Adagi.	Dishonest; roguish.
Pizwi.	Futile; senseless.
Kpagi.	Thick.
Wazabi.	Thin.
Tkuigui.	Heavy.
Tatebi.	Level; even; alike.
Abagi.	Flat.

NOTE.—All the above adjectives signify nothing by themselves; they signify what is ascribed to them, but when they are prolonged by someother syllables; as, *go, gen,* etc., etc., or connected with someother words, either nouns or verbs. They are therefore invariable, being in somehow but particles of words.

THE FOREGOING ADJECTIVES

Prolonged by syllables representing the verb *to be,* and
joined to nouns and verbs in the affirmative and negative form,
either with or without interrogation.

Wligo.	1	He, she, (it) is good.
Wligen.	7	It is good.
Wligeɯ?	7	Is it good?
Kehi sibo, (or kchitegw).	5	A great river.
Msinôguat?		Does it look big?
Mamsi ki.		A vast ground.
Wski alnôba.	4	A young man.
Wski wigwôm, (or wski gamigw).		A new house.
N'manohom negôni paskhigan.		I buy an old gun.
N-d-agidam Wawasi Awighigan.		I read the Bible, (*lit.* the holy book).
Sôgmôwi Pial.		St. Peter.
Pili kisos.		The new moon.
Pildowi ôjmowôgan.		A new history.
Wôbigen?	7	Is it white?
Wôbigen.	7	It is white.
Wôbigo.	1	He (she) is white.

Mkazawigo.	1	He (she) is black.
Mkazawigen.	7	It is black.
Sôgli sanôba.	1	A stout man.
Mlikigo.	1	He, she, (it) is strong.
Nokigen.	7	It is soft.
Pôgui môniiô.	8	Of pure (of solid) silver.
Adagi pmôwsowinno.	1	A dishonest person.
Pizwi klosowôgan.	5	A vain talk, a futile argument.
Kpagizo pkuami.		The ice is thick.
W'meljassa wazabizoa.		His (her) mittens are thin.
Tkwguinôgwat.	7	It looks heavy.
Tkwguinôgwzo.	1	He, she,(it) looks heavy.
O'da tatebigenowial.		They are not alike.
Abagigen k'-d-a b a z-noda?		Is your basket flat?
Abagigen n'-d-a b a z noda.		My basket is flat.

VOCABULARY OF ADJECTIVES.

(Contracted and Variable).

Waligit. Waligek. }	Good, handsome.
Majigit. Majigek. }	Bad, wicked, mean.
Masgilek. Masguikwek. }	Great, large, big.
Piwsessit. Piwsessek. }	Little, small.
Wskia.	New.
Negônia.	Old.
Wôbigit. Wôbigek. }	White.
Makazawigit. Makazawigek. }	Black.
Sôglizit. Sôglak. }	Solid, strong, durable
Malkigit. Malkigek. }	Strong, stout.

Nokigit. Nokigek. }	Soft, tender.
Pôguigit. Pôguigek. }	Pure, genuine.
Sasagigit. Sasagigek. }	Straight.
Piziwadoit. Piziwadoik. }	Useless, void, futile.
Kapagizit. Kapagak. }	Thick.
Wazabizit, Wazabak. }	Thin.
Takwiguelek. Takwiguak. }	Heavy.
Abagigit,[1] Abagigek. }	Flat.

THE FOREGOING ADJECTIVES

JOINED TO NOUNS, EITHER SINGULAR OR PLURAL.

(Simple and Contracted).

Wli ases.	A good horse.
Wli kaoz*ak.*	Good cows.
Waligijik ases*ak.*	Fine horses.
Waligek wigwôm.	A fine house.
Walikkil tasakuabon*al.*	Fine (good) chairs.
Majiwskinnosis.	A bad boy, a mean lad.
Majigit aples.	A bad apple, (unsound).
Majikk*il* pilaskwimôni*al.*	The counterfeit bank notes.
Kchi nebes*al.*	Great lakes.

---

1. NOTE.—As there are in Abenakis *two* kinds of Substantives, viz: the *animate*, denoting objects having *animal life;* and the *inanimate*, denoting inanimate objects; so also there are *animate* and *inanimate* Adjectives and Verbs, which are made to agree with the substantives accordingly. Those substantives are distinguished by the termination of the *plural*, which is always *k* for the *animate*, (as well as for the *personified*, which are treated as if they were *animate*), and *l* for the *inanimate*. We likewise distinguish the *adjectives* by their termination in the *singular*, which is usually, as above, *k* for the *animate*, and *l* for the *inanimate*.

Masegilek wdahôgan.	A long (large) paddle.
Maseguikwk*il* kikôn*al*.	Large fields.
Piwsessij*ik* alemoss*ak*.	Little dogs.
Piwsessek nbizonkikôn.	A small garden.
Wski peljes.	A new pair pants, a new pantaloon.
Wski ôbagawatahigan.	A new umbrella.
Negôni wlômawaldamwôgan.	A superstition, (literally: an old imagination).
Wôbigit azib.	A white sheep.
Wobikkil masksa*al*.	White blankets.
Makazawigit skuôzontagw.	Some black thread.
Makazawigek silki.	Some black silk;——ribbon.
Sôglizit wakôlihws.	A strong cart;—wheel.
Sôglak wagin.	A strong waggon.
Malkigit sanôba; maliksanit—.	A stout man; a strong—.
Malkigek *or* maliksanoik kadosmowôgan.	Spirituous liquor, (literally: strong beverage).
Nokigit pohkuasimon.	A soft pillow.
Nokigek abazi.	Some soft wood.
Pôgui alnôbak.	Full blooded indians.
Pizwadoit nodalokat.	A heartless servant.
Pizwadoik alokawogan	A fruitless labour.
Kapagizijik meljassak.	Thick mittens.
Kapagakil mkezenal.	Thick moccasins, or shoes.
Wazabizit madagen.	A thin hide.
Wazabagil medasal.	Thin socks.
Takwiguelek nidazo.	A heavy animal.
Takwiguak ôbadahon.	A heavy cane.
Abagigijik potôiiak.	Flat bottles.
Abagigek abaznoda.	A flat basket.

SENTENCES EXEMPLIFYING

The foregoing Nouns and Adjectives, either in the affirmative, negative, or interrogative form.

N'wajônô wli ases.	I have a good horse.
O'da wajônawi wli kaoza.	He (she) has no good cows.

K'wajônôbena waligijik asesak? — Have we some good horses?
K'manohomebaji walikkil wigwômal. — You will buy fine (good) houses.

Wlitoakba walikkil tasakwabonal. — They would make fine chairs.
O'da n'kezalmôw maji wskinnisisak. — I don't like bad boys.

O'da k'dachwalmôw maji aplesak? — Don't you want some bad apples?
O'daaba wdenmowi maji pilaskwimônial. — He would not take the conterfeit bank notes.

'Namito kchi nebesal. — He (she) sees some great lakes.
W'namitonal kchi nebesal. — He (she) sees the great lakes.
K'kiz'ônkolhôn masegilek wdahôgan? — Have you (thou) sold the large paddle?
K'kiz'ônkolhônal maseguikwkil kikônal. — Have you (thou) sold the large fields?
N'nanawalmônnawkji piwsessijik alemossak. — We will keep the little dogs.

K'-d-asamôwôkba alemossisak? — Would you feed the little dogs?——the puppies?

W'-d-ôpchi nokapodonal piwsessekil nbizonkikônal. — He (she) is harrowing the small gardens.
N'kiz'ônkolhô wski peljes. — I have sold a new pantaloon.
O'da k'waniadow wski ôbagawatahigan? — Did not you lose a new umbrella?

Kaguessi negôni wlômawaldamwôgan ni? — What a superstition is that?

N'nihlô wôbigit azib. — I killed the white sheep.
Awakatoak wôbikkil masksaal. — They use white blankets.
N'-d-achoalmô skuôsontagw wôbigit. — I want some white thread.

N'-d-achoaldam silki wôbigek. — I want some white silk.
K'-d-alokamibesa sôglizit wakôlikws? — Did you order a strong cart?

N'-d-alokamib sôglak wagin. — I ordered a strong waggon.
N'-d-ôgazahôbenaba malkigit sanôba. — We would hire a stout man.

K'wikuenembenaba (malkigek) kadosmowôgan. — We would take some (spirituous) liquor.
N'wajônô nokigit pohkuasimon. — I have a soft pillow.

N'wajônem nokigek abazi.	I have some soft wood.
Pôgui alnôbak kiuwô?	Are you full blooded indians?
Pôgui alnôbak niuna.	We are full blooded indians.
O'do niuna pôgui alnôbak.	We are not full blooded indians.
O'da n'-d-achwalmôw pizwadoit nodalokad.	I don't want a heartless servant.
'Wlito pizwadoik alokawôgan.	He (she) makes a useless work.
O'pchito pizwadoik alokawôgan.	He (she) is making a useless work.
K'kiz'anohôk kapagizijik meljassak?	Did you buy the thick mittens?
K'kiz'anohobmebesa kapagakil mkezenal?	Did you buy some thick moccasins?
N'manohôba wazabisijik madagenok.	I should buy some thin hides.

OF NUMBERS.

(1. *Cardinal numbers*).

1 Pazekw. ⎫	
2 Pazego. ⎬	One.
3 Pazegwen. ⎭	
1 Nis. ⎫	
2 Nisoak. ⎬	Two.
3 Nisnol. ⎭	
1 Nas. ⎫	
2 Nloak. ⎬	Three.
3 Nhenol. ⎭	
1 Iaw. ⎫	
2 Iawak. ⎬	Four
3 Iawnol. ⎭	
1 Nôlan. ⎫	
2 Nonnoak. ⎬	Five.
3 Nonnenol. ⎭	

OBSERVATION.—Cardinal numbers from one to five, as above, are of three kinds, viz: 1. *Abstract* numbers or those used merely in counting: *pazekw, nis, nas,* etc., one, two, three, etc; 2. *Concrete* numbers or those pertaining to the limitation of the *animate* objects, and *personified* things; as, *pazego sanôba*, one man; *nisoak môniak*, two dollars; 3. *Concrete* numbers used to determine things only; as, *pazegwen awighigan*, one book; *nônnenol wigwômal*, live houses.

Nguedôz.	Six.
Tôbawôz.	Seven.
Nsôzek.	Eight.
Noliwi.	Nine.
Mdala.	Ten.
Nguedonkaw,	Eleven.
Nisônkaw.	Twelve.
Nsônkaw. (*pron: cow*).	Thirteen.
Iawônkaw.	Fourteen.
Nônônkaw.	Fifteen.
Nguedôz kasônkaw.	Sixteen.
Tôbanôz kasônbaw.	Seventeen.
Nsôzek kasônkaw.	Eighteen.
Noliwi kasônkaw.	Nineteen.
Nisinska.	Twenty.
Nisinska taba pazekw.	Twenty-one.
Nisinska taba nis.	Twenty-two.
Nisinska taba nas.	Twenty-three.
Nisinska taba iaw.	Twenty-four.
Nisinska taba nôlan.	Twenty-five.
Nisinska taba nguedôz.	Twenty-six.
Nisinska taba tôbawôz.	Twenty-seven.
Nisinska taba nsôzek.	Twenty-eight.
Nisinska taba noliwi.	Twenty-nine.
Nsinska.	Thirty.
Nsinska taba pazekw, etc.	Thirty-one, etc.
Iawinska.	Fourty.
Iawinska taba pazekw, etc.	Fourty-one, etc.
Nônninska.	Fifty.
Nônninska taba pazekw, etc.	Fifty-one, etc.
Nguedôz kasinska.	Sixty
Nguedôz kasinska taba pazekw, etc.	Sixty-one, etc.
Tôbawôz kasinska.	Seventy.
Tôbawôz kasinska taba pazekw, etc.	Seventy-one, etc.
Nsôzek kasinska.	Eighty.
Nsôzek kasinska taba pazekw, etc.	Eighty-one, etc.
Noliwi kasinska.	Ninety.

Noliwi kasinska taba pazekw, etc.	Ninety-one, etc.
Nguedatgua.	One hundred.
Nguedatgua taba pazekw, etc.	Hundred and one, etc.
Nisatgua.	Two hundred.
Nisatgua taba pazekw, etc.	Two hundred and one, etc.
Nsatgua.	Three hundred.
Nsatgua taba pazekw, etc.	Three hundred and one, etc.
Iawatgua.	Four hundred.
Iawatgua taba pazekw, etc.	Four hundred and one, etc.
Nônnatgua.	Five hundred.
Nônnatgua taba pazekw, etc.	Five hundred and one, etc.
Nguedôz kasatgua.	Six hundred.
Nguedôz kasatgua taba pazekw, etc.	Six hundred and one, etc.
Tôbawôz kasatgua.	Seven hundred.
Tôbawôz kazatgua taba pazekw, etc.	Seven hundred and one, etc.
Nsôzek kasatgua.	Eight hundred.
Nsôzek kasatgua taba pazekw, etc.	Eight hundred and one, etc.
Noliwi kasatgua.	Nine hundred.
Noliwi kasatgua taba pazekw, etc.	Nine hundred and one, etc.
Nguedômkuaki. (pron.—ak—ki).	One thousand.
Nisômkuaki taba nis.	Two thousand and two. etc.
Nsômkuaki taba nas.	Three thousand and three.
Iawômkuaki taba iaw.	Four thousand and four.
Nônnômkuaki taba nôlan.	Five thousand and five.
Nguedôz kasômkuaki.	Six thousand.
Tôbawôz kasômkuaki.	Seven thousand.
Mdala kasômkuaki.	Ten thousand.
Nguedatgua kasômkuaki.	Hundred thousand.
Nônnatgua kasômkuaki.	Five hundred thousand.
Kehi-nguedômkuaki.	One million.
Nisda kehi-nguedômkuaki.	Two millions.
Mdala kasta kchi-ngue- dômkuaki.	Ten millions.

(2. *Distributive numbers*).

Papazego; papazegwen.	One by one; one each, or to each.
Nenisoak; nenisnol.	Two everytime, three each, or to each.

Nenloak; nenhenol.	3 everytime, 3 each, or to each.
Ieiawak; ieiawnol.	4 everytime, 4 each, or to each.
Nenônnoak; nenônnenol.	5 everytime, 5 each, or to each.
Nenguedôz.	6 everytime, 6 each, or to each.
Tetôbawôz.	7 everytime, 7 each, or to each.
Nensôzek.	8 everytime, 8 each, or to each.
Nenoliwi.	9 everytime, 9 each, or to each.
Memdala.	10 everytime, 10 each, or to each.
Nenguedônkaw.	11 everytime, 11 each, or to each.
Nenisônkaw.	12 everytime, 12 each, or to each.
Nensônkaw.	13 everytime, 13 each, or to each.
leïawônkaw.	14 everytime, 14 each, or to each.
Nenônnônkaw.	15 everytime, 15 each, or to each.
Nenguedôz kasônkaw.	16 everytime, 16 each, or to each.
Tetôbawôz kasônkaw.	17 everytime, 17 each, or to each.
Nensôzek kasônkaw.	18 everytime, 18 each, or to each.
Nenoliwi kasônkaw.	19 everytime, 19 each, or to each.
Neuisinska.	20 everytime, 20 each, or to each.
Nenisinska taba pazekw.	21 everytime, 21 each, or to each.
Nensinska.	30 everytime, 30 each, or to each.
Nensinska taba pazekw.	31 everytime, 31 each, or to each.
Ieiawinska.	40 everytime, 40 each, or to each.
Nenônniska.	50 everytime, 50 each, or to each.
Neneguedôz kasinska.	60 everytime, 60 each, or to each.
Tetôbawôz kasinska.	70 everytime, 70 each, or to each.
Nensôzek kasinska.	80 everytime, 80 each, or to each.
Nenoliwi kasinska.	90 everytime, 90 each, or to each.
Nenguedatgua.	100 everytime, 100 each, or to each.
Nenguedalgua taba pazekw.	101 everytime, 101 each, or to each.
Nenisatgua.	200 everytime, 200 each, or to each.
Nensatgua.	300 everytime, 300 each, or to each.
Ieiawatgua.	400 everytime, 400 each, or to each.
Nenoliwi kasatgua.	900 everytime, 900 each, or to each.

Nenguedômkuaki.	1000 everytime, 1000 each, or to each.
Nenisômkuaki.	2000 everytime, 2000 each, or to each.
Nensômkuaki.	3000 everytime, 3000 each, or to each.
Nenguedôz kasômkuaki.	6000 everytime, 6000 each, or to each.
Nenoliwi kasômkuaki.	9000 everytime, 9000 each, or to each.
Memdala kasômkuaki.	10,000 everytime, 10,000 each, or to each.
Nenisinska kasômkuaki.	20,000 everytime, 20,000 each, or to each.
Nenguedatgua kasômkuaki.	100,000 everytime, 100,000 each, or to each.
Kekchi nguedômkuaki.	1,000,000 everytime, 1,000,000 each, or to each.

(3. *Multiplying Numbers*).

Pazgueda.	Once.
Nisda.	Twice.
Nseda.	Three times.
Iawda.	Four times.
Nônneda.	Five times.
Nguedôz kasta.	6 times.
Tôbawôz kasta.	7 "
Nsôzek kasta.	8 "
Noliwi kasta.	9 "
Mdala kasta.	10 "
Nguedônkaw kasta.	11 "
Nonnônkaw kasta.	15 "
Noliwi kasônkaw kasta	19 "
Nisinska kasta.	20 "
Nisinska taba pazekw kasta.	21 "
Nisinska taba nis kasta.	22 "
Nsinska kasta.	30 "
Nsinska taba nôlan kasta.	35 "

Iawinska kasta.	40 times.
Nônninska kasta.	50 "
Nguedatgua kasta.	100 "
Nguedoz kasatgua kasta.	600 "
Nguedômkuaki kasta.	1000 "
Kehi-nguedomkuaki taba neguedôz kasatgua taba nônninska taba nôlan kasta.	1000,655 " (*Literally*: one great thousand and six hundred and fifty and five times).

(4. *Multiplying-Distributive Numbers*).

Papazgueda.	Once very time; once each, or to each.
Nenisda.	Twice everytime; twice each, or to each.
Nenseda.	Three times everytime, 3 times each, or to each.
Ieiawda.	4 times everytime; 4 times each, or to each.
Nenônneda.	5 times everytime; 5 times each or to each.
Nenguedôz kasta.	6 times everytime; 6 times each, or to each.
Tetôbawoz kasta.	7 times everytime; 7 times each, or to each.
Nensôzek kasta.	8 times everytime; 8 times each or to each.
Nenoliwi kasta.	9 times everytime; 9 times each, or to each.
Memdala kasta.	10 times everytime; 10 times each, or to each.
Nenizônkaw kasta.	12 times everytime; 12 times each, or to each.
Nenônnônkaw kasta.	15 times everytime; 15 times each, or to each.
Nenisinska kasta.	20 times everytime; 20 times each, or to each.

Nenisinska taba pazekw kasta.	21 times everytime; 21 times each, or to each.
Nensinska kasta.	30 times everytime; 30 times each, or to each.
Ieiawinska kasta.	40 times everytime; 40 times each, or to each.
Nenônninska kasta.	50 times everytime; 50 times each, or to each.
Nenguedatgua kasta.	100 times everytime; 100 times each, or to each.
Nenisatgua kasta.	200 times everytime; 200 times each, or to each.
Nenônnatgua kasta.	500 times everytime; 500 times each, or to each.
Nenguedômkuaki kasta.	1000 times everytime; 1000 times each, or to each.

(5. *Ordinal numbers marking the order and succession of animate objects, and personified things*).

Nitamabit.	The first.
Nis akwôbabit.	The second.
Nas akwôbabit.	The third.
Iaw akwôbabit.	The fourth.
Nôlan akwôbabit.	The fifth.
Mdala akwôbabit.	The tenth.
Nônnônkaw akwôbtak.	The fifteenth.
Nguedôz kasônkaw akwôbauit.	The sixteenth.
Nisinska akwôbabit.	The twentieth.
Iawinska akwôbabit.	The fortieth.
Nôninska akwôbabit.	The fiftieth.
Nguedôz kasinska akwôbabit.	The sixtieth.
Noliwi kasinska akwôbabit.	The ninetieth.
Noliwi kasinska taba noliwi akwôbabit.	The ninety-ninth.
Nguedatgua akwôbabit.	The hundreth.
Nguedatgua taba nônninska kwôbabit.	The hundred and fiftieth.

Nguedômkuaki taba nonnatgua taba nônninska taba nôlan akwôbabit, etc., etc.	The thousand five hundred and fifty-fifth, etc., etc.

(6. *Ordinal numbers marking the order and succession of things*).

Nitamatak.	The first.
Nis akwôbtak.	The second.
Nas akwôbtak.	The third.
Iaw akwôbtak.	The fourth.
Nôlan akwôbtak.	The fifth.
Mdala akwôbtak.	The tenth.
Nônnônkaw akwôbtak.	The fifteenth.
Nguedôz kasônkaw akwôbtak.	The sixteenth.
Nisinska akwôbtak.	The twentieth.
Iawinska akwôbtak.	The fortieth.
Nônninska akwôbtak.	The fiftieth.
Nguedôz kasinska akwôbtak.	The sixtieth.
Noliwi kasinska taba noliwi akwôbtak.	The ninety-ninth.
Nguedatgua taba nônninska akwôbtak.	The hundred and fiftieth.
Mdala kasômkuaki taba nônnatgua taba nônninska taba nôlan akwôbtak, etc.	The ten thousand five hundred and fifty fifth, etc.

(7. *Ordinal numbers marking the order and succession of chapters, verses, sections of laws, articles of regulations, etc*).

Nitamagimguak *or* pazekw alagimguak.	First.
Nis alagimguak.	Second, or secondly.
Nas alagimguak.	Third, or thirdly.
Nôlan alagimguak.	Fifth, or fifthly.
Mdala alagimguak.	Tenth, or tenthly.
Nisinska alagimguak.	Twentieth, or twentiethly.
Nônninska alagimguak.	Fiftieth, or fiftiethly.
Nguedatgua alagimguak, etc., etc.	Hundreth, or hundredthly, etc., etc.

Iawi chebenôzik.	One quarter.
Psigia; pabasi...	The half.
Iawi chebonozik nsichebat.	Three quarters; three fourths.
Nasi chebenôzik.	The third.
Nasi chebenôzik nisichebat.	Two thirds.
Nônni chebenôzik.	One fifth.
Nônni chebenôzik nsichebat.	Three fifths.
Nguedôz kasi chebenôzik.	One sixth.
Mdala kasi chebenôzik.	One tenth.
Mdala kasi chebenôzik iawi-chebat.	Four tenths.
Nguedatgua kasi chebenôzik, etc.	One hundredth, etc.

(9. *Multiple numbers*).

Pkawiwi. (or nisda pkawiwi).	The double.
Nseda pkawiwi.	The triple.
Iawdi pkawiwi.	The quadruple.
Nônneda pkawiwi.	The quintuple.
Nguedatgua kasta pkawiwi.	The centuple.

VOCABULARY OF ADVERBS, PREPOSITIONS, CONJUNCTIONS AND INTERJECTIONS.

INVARIABLE PARTICLES.

(1. *Adverbs*).

O'hôô.	Yes.
Kalaata.	Indeed; truly; in fact.
O'da.	No; not; neither, nor.
Kizi.	Already; after.
Mina.	Again, yet, still.
Askua.	Still, again.
Asma.	Never, not yet.
Kigizi.	Already; beforehand.
Wlôgwa.	Yesterday.

Saba.	Tomorrow.
Pita.	Very, much.
Nopaiwi.	Far.
Pasojiwi.	Near; nearly.
Tôni.	How; where; what.
Tôni kasi...	How much.
Mawia.	Better.
Awasiwi.	Beyond, furthermore.
Chitôiwi, (chito...)	Further; worst.
Nodôiwi, (nodô...)	Less.
Tagasiwi, (tagasi...)	Little; few.
Wigawôjiwi, (wigawôji...)	Often, frequently.
Sipkiwi, (sipki...)	Late.
Nadawiwi, (nadawi...)	Seldom, rarely.
Nabiwi, (nabi...)	Early, soon.
Mamlawiwi. (mamlawi...)	Much; abundantly.
Sasagiwi, (sasagi...)	Straight, directly.
Nitta.	Forthwith, immediately.
Pasodawiwi.	Near, nearly.
Pabômiwi.	About.
Ni.	So; and.
Kwaskuai.	Enough.
(Wami..., tabi...)	Enough.
Wzômi.	Too much.
Mina.	More; again.
Askua awasiwi.	Furthermore, moreover
(Kassi...)	So much, so many.
Nôbi kassi.	As much, as many.
Alwa.	Almost.
U, iu, u tali.	Here.
Ni, enni, ni tali.	There.
Kizi.	Already.
Almitebihlôk.	Afterwards.
Askua mina.	Yet, still yet.
Chiga.	When.
Ni, ni adoji.	Then.
Nôwat, negôniwi.	Formerly.
Wskebi, kizilla.	Perhaps.
Wigôdamiwi, (wigôdami...)	Willingly.

Kassiwi.	Together.
Pabômiwi.	About.
Nalwiwi.	Everywhere.
Paliwi.	Elsewhere.
Kwajemiwi.	Out; outside.
Chebiwi.	Besides.
Kwelbiwi.	Behind.
Awasiwi.	Beyond, over.
Nikuôbioji.	Henceforth, hereafter.
Tasiwi.	Upon.
Wazwawi, (wazwa...)	Back, backward.
Nikôniwi, (nikôni...[1])	Ahead, forward.

(2. *Prepositions*).

Asma awdimokw.	Before the war.
Kisi spôzikimuk.	After breakfast.
Nikôniwi agmak.	Before him.
Kasiwi wijiaa.	With is brother.
Kikajiwi chebessagahiganek.	Against the wall.
Alômiwi ababskedak.	In the stove.
Oji papaiôda.	Since his arrival.
Kwelbiwi klôganek.	Behind the door.
Wskijiwi tawipodik.	On the table.
Naguiwi abonek.	Under the bed.
Nansawiwi tawzôganikok.	Between the windows.
Laguiwi niak.	Towards me.
Chebiwi awôssisak.	Besides the children.
Weji môni.	For cash.
Kwani podawazimuk.	During the council.
Akuôbi kistôzik.	According the decision.
Akuôbigek chowagidamwôganal.	According the commandments.
Wskijiwi abakuôganek.	Upon the roof.
Weji ni lidwôgan.	Concerning (for) that affair.
Pabômiwi, nisoak môniak.	About two dollars.

---

1. NOTE. These *adverbs* placed between *parenthesis* mean what is ascribed to them but when they are placed before a verb, or an adjective, and never can be used otherwise: *Nikôni môjob*, he (she) went ahead.

Sôbiwi whagak.	Through the body.
Wiwniwi wigwômek.	Round the house.
Pasodawiwi *or* pasojiwi niunak.	Near us.
Sebôiwi *or* aseboiwi pemelodigan.	Along the fence.
Kuajemiwi aiamihawigamigok.	Out of the church.
Tatebesbawiwi odanak.	Opposite the city.
Weji nia.	As for me, for me, for my part.
Lli asokwek.	Up to the clouds.
Awasiwi odanak.	Beyond the city, village.
Pôzijiwi ni.	Above that,—place.

(3. *Conjunctions*).

Ta, ni.	And; also.
Achi.	Also.
Kôdak.	Thus; as.
Wzômi.	For, because.
Oji ali.	Whereas; because.
Kanwa.	But; however.
Taôlawi.	As; like.
Ni nawa.	Therefore, then.
Tôni adoji.	When.
O'da.	Nor.
Chaga.	If.
Tôni.	Whether, if.
Kanwa.	Nevertheless.
Ali.	That; because.
Minaguiba.	Though, although.
Waji; wajiji.	That, in order that.
Pajitebihlôga.	In case, if.
Ni wattak.	Therefore; wherefore.
Weji alinsatôzik.	For fear that.
Tabat, tabatta.	Provided that.
O'daki.	Rather than.
Aiaga; chaga ôda.	Unless.
Anegitta.	As soon as.
Nôbi taôlawi.	As well as, in the same way as.
Oji ali.	As; because.
Oji ali nsatôzik.	For fear that.

Tabat.	Provided that.
Kaalaki.	Indeed, in reality.

(4. *Interjections*).

Ahaa!	
Enni!	
Iahi!	Exclamations expressing success and satisfaction.
Wligen!	
Aiioo!	
Akkwajala!	
Kaamôji!	Articulations expressing embarrassment.
Niaiaga!	
Saaginôgw!	
Kdemôginôgw!	
Wessaginôgw!	Articulations expressing commiseration or pity.
Saagad!	
O'galiguômuk!	
Wha!	
Nha!	Exclamations expressing derision or irony.
Kamôji!	
Alliguanôgw!	
Ah!	
Aie!	Exclamations expressing disapprobation.
Aah!	
Sh't!	Articulations commanding silence.
Tabat!	

FAMILIAR PHRASES TO FACILITATE CONVERSATION.

(1. *For questioning, affirming, denying, going, coming, etc.*)

Awani na?	Who is that?
Nmitogwes na.	That's my father.
Kagui *or* Kagwes ni?	What is that?
Wizôwimônii sakhiljahon.	A gold ring.
Tôni k'-d-lanohomen ni sakhiljahon?	How much did you pay for that ring?

Nônnoak môniak.	Five dollars.
Kagui lla?	What is the matter?
Nawji papoldoak, ketagik awdoldoak.	Some are playing, the others are fighting.
Kagui llitôguat?	What is the news?
O'da kagui nôdamiwi.	Nothing particular.
Chiga paiôan? (sing.)	When did you come? (arrive?)
Wlôgwa or wlôgoa.	Yesterday.
Kagui askawitoan?	What are you Waiting for?
N'd-askawiton n'mônim.	I am waiting for my money.
Kagui k'-d-eliwizi?	What is your name?
N'-d-eliwizi Sozap.	My name is Joseph.
Kagui k'-d-idam?	What do you say?
Odatta n'keloziw.	I don't speak at all.
Kagui k'-d-elaloka? (sing.)	What are you doing? (sing.)
Kagui k'-d-elalokaba? (daul.)	What are you doing? (dual.)
Kagui k'-d-elalokhediba? (plur.)	What are you doing? (plur.)
N'-d-abaznodakabena.[1]	We are making baskets.
N'-d-abaznodakhcdibena.	We are making baskets.
Kagui kadi nadodemawian?	What do you want to ask me?
K'kadi nadodemol waji nadmihian nlhoak môniak.	I want to ask you to lend me three dollars.
Awani u wigwôm?	Whose house is this?
Awani u wigit?	Who lives here?
Nmessis.	My sister (older than I).
Nichenis.	My brother. ⎫ My sister. ⎬ (younger than I).
Awani ulil w'-d-awikhiganal?	Whose books are these?
Awani nilil w'pilaskomal?	Whose papers are those?
Nidôpso ulil w'-d-awikhiganal.	These books are my sister's— belong to my sister.
Nitsakaso nilil w'pilaskomal.	Those papers belong to my sister.
Kagui n'-d-achowi llalokabena?	What have we to do?

---

1. *N'-d-abaznodakabena* is generally used when speaking of two or more persons, if their number is definite to the speaker; but when he has no definite idea of the number of persons performing the action, he will say: *n'dabaznodakhedibena*, we (many of us) make baskets.

Kagui k'-d-achowi llalokabena?[1]	What have we to do?
K'-d-achowi môjibna kpiwi.	We have to go into the woods.
Awani kwilawahoan?	Whom do you look for?
Kagui kwilawatoan?	What do you look for?
Kagui waniadoan?	What have you lost?
N'moswa n'waniadon.	I lost my handkerchief, (lit: my handkerchief I lost it).
N'waniado môni	I lost some money.
N'waniadon moni.	I lost the money.
Ni alak. Lla ni.	It is the truth. It is true.
K'kizi wlômawaldamikhoga.	You have been imposed upon.
Akui nitta wlômawalma mziwi awani.	Don't believe immediately everybody.
Alni ni k'-d-idamen?	Do you joke?
O'da k'olômawalmelo.	I don't believe you.
K'olôma; wlôma.	You are in the right; he is in the right.
O'da wlômawi; ôda wlômawiak.	He (she) is not in the right; they are not in the right.
Wzômi kelozo.	He (she) speaks too much.
Wzômi msôdoak.	They speak too loud.
Sôgnawabigw; k'ozômi nesktôgwziba.	Be quiet; you make too much noice. (pl.)
K'wawinawôwô na sanôba?	Do you know that man? (plur.)
N'wanaldamen w'wizowôgan.	I forgot his name.
O'da tabinôguatowi ni tbelodôzo.	It is not worth while to speak of that.
N'-d-achewaldamen k'olitawin. . .	I want you to make me. . .
Wliwni wji k'olidahawôgan nia wji.	I thank you for your kindness towards me.
K'ozômi wlidahô nia wji.	You are too good to me.
N'olilawakôgon ni n'-d-elalokan kia weji.	It affords me pleasure to do that for you. (sing.)
Tôni alosaan.	Where are you going? (sing.)
Tôni alosaak.	Where are you going? (plur.)

---

1. Here *we* includes the person or persons to whom the interrogation is made; whereas in the preceding sentence, *we* excludes the person or persons spoken to; as given in the *article* of *pronouns*, at the end of the First Part of this book.

Nopaiwi n'-d-elosa.	I am going far—. off.
O'daaba k'kizi wijawiw	You can't come with me. (sing.)
Pasojiwi n'-d-elesa.	I am going near by.
Wijawigw.	Come with me (plur.)
N'môgi wigiak.	I am going home.
'Môjo wigiidit.	He (she) is going home.
'Môjoak wigiidit.	They are going home.
K'ozômi kezosaba.	You walk too fast. (pl.)
Wzômi mannosak.	They walk too slow.
K'wizaka?	Are you in a great hurry? (sing.)
Llosada agômek.	Let us go to the other side of the river.
Pkagônda, (lessaguôgan, sibo, ôwdi, etc.)	Let us cross, (the bridge, the river, the road, etc.)
Pidigada.	Let us go in.
Sahosada.	Let us go out.
Sahosagw.	Go out. (plur.)
N'-d-aspigôdawa.	I go up (stairs).
N'penôdawa.	I go down (stairs).
U llagosada.	Let us go this way.
Ni alagosaadit.	They go that way.
Lagosa alnakaiwi (*ind.* and *imp.*)	He (she) goes to the right; go to the right.
O'da llagosawi pôjiwi.	He (she) does not go to the left.
Sôsasagosatta (*imp.* and *ind.*)	Go straight along; he (she) goes straight along.
Wazwassa tagasiwi, (*imp.* and *ind.*)	Go back a little (sing.) he (she) goes back a little.
Petegi mina.	Go back again (sing).
Akui môji, ôai u kasiwi niuna.	Don't go away, stay here with us.
Tôni wadosaan? (*sg.*) } Toni wadosaakw? (*pl.*) }	Where do you come from?
N'odosa k'wigwômwôg	I come from your house.
N'odosa wigiak.	I come from home.
N'odosa nzasisek.*	I come from my uncle's
Losa ni.	Go there, (sing.)

---

* See the explanations concerning the terms of relationship page 26.

Wijawi, (sing.) }
Wijawigw, (plur.) }

Come (along) with me.

Pasodosa skwedak, awazi.

Come near the fire, warmed yourself.

K'-d-askawiholji.

I will wait for you, (sing.)

Skawihigw u tali.

Wait for me here, (sing.)

Tôwdana klôgan, tawzôgan.

Open the door, the window, (sing.)

Kebaha klôganal ta tawzôganal.

Shut the doors and the windows.

N'môji wigiak nikwôbi.

I go home now.

Sabaji u mina n'paiôn.

Tomorrow I will come here again (*lit.* tomorrow will here again I come at).

Nôbitta ni talebat w'paiôn ala ôda.

It is all the same whether he comes or not.

K'tabinôgwzinô k'sazamhoganô.

You deserve to be whipped. (pl.)

Mamagahôbnnik weji pôbatamwôgan.

They have been ill treated for religion's sake.

K'-d-akwamalsoinôgwzi.

You look sick.

Pazego ôpdalmo, kedak melisja.

One laughs, and the other weeps.

Azô paami wawôdam ôdaki Pial.

John is wiser than Peter.

Wilawigoak tatebiwi.

They are both rich.

Saagigoak tatebiwi?

Are the both industrious?

Saagigoak tatebiwi.

They are both industrious.

Nôbi w'toji wilawigin tahôlawi widokana.

He (she) is as rich as his (her) brother.

Kakaswi almi kchiaooit, kakaswi kagapsa.

The older he (she) grows, the deafer he (she) is.

Kakaswi almi alokaa, kakaswi n'olôwzi.

The more I work, the better off I am.

Tôniji kwani wlideb'alokaa n'kezalmegwziji.

As long as I shall behave well, I will be loved.

O'da n'tabi wilawigiw waji ni manohoma.

I am not rich enough to buy that.

Paami nabi paiak pamekisgak ôdaki attoji paiôdit.

They arrived today sooner than they usually do.

K'mamlawi nodôsani ôdaki agma.

You are by far not so strong as he is.

N'-d-eliwlaldamawôn w'-d-elosan kpiwi.

I give him leave to go to the woods.

Kakaswi kagapsa almi kchaioit.	The older he grows, the deafer he is.
Kakaswi n' - d - aloka, kaswi n'saagôwzi.	The more I work, the more needy I am.
Azo adali wawinak weji mziwi agakimogik.	John is the most advanced of all my scholars.

(2. To inquire after health).

Paakuinôgwzian, nijia.	Good morning, Sir[1].
Tôni k-d-ôllôwzin?	How do you do?
N'wôwlôwzi pita.	Very well, (lit: I am very well).
Tôni k-d-awôssissemak w'-d-ôllôwzinô?	How do your children do?
Wôwlôwzoak mziwi.	They are all well.
Tôni kigawes w'd-ôllôwzin?	How does your mother do?
O'da kuina wôwlôwziwi.	She is not (very) well.
Kagui lôwza?	What is her illness? (what ails her?)
Wesguinôgana mzena.	She has got a cold.
N'-d-elsedam knôjikw agua achi mômadamalso.	I have heard your uncle is also unwell.
Llaki ni, w'kuedôgan w'-d-akuamadamen.	So it is, he has got a sore throat.
Nôwat wa awôssis w'noji akwamalsin?	Has this child been sick now a long time?
O'da kuina nôwat.	No, not very long.
K'wajônem nbizonal.	Have you any medicines?
N'mesalto wli nbizonal.	I have many good medicines.
N'wigôdam ni alsedolan.	I am happy to hear you say so.

(3. Of the Age).

K'kasigadema?	How old are you?
Nisinska n'kasigadema.	I am twenty years old.
Kasigademak kmitôgwes ta kigawes?	How old are your father and your mother?

---

1. NOTE.—*Nijia* (*my* brother) is used instead of *Sir* in English.

Abenaki	English
Nmitôgwes nguedôz kasinska kasigadema, ni nigawes nônninska.	My father is sixty years old, and my mother fifty.
Pita kizi kchiaoo nmitô gwes.	My father is already very old.
Nigawes paami kchiainôgwezo ôdaki kasigademad.	My mother looks older than she is.
Wski alnôbao; wski phanemoo.	He is a young man; she is a young woman.
Askua pita k'nahnôgamato, ôlawi pita k'kichiawwi.	You are yet active (vigorous), although very old
N'-d-alamizowi wahwôgomô Tabaldak milit sôglamalsowôgan akwôbigademaa.	I thank the Lord who gives me good health in my age.
K'kasigadema tahôlawi nia?	Are you of my age?
N'kasigadema tahôlawi kia, tahôlawi agma.	I am of your age, of his age.
Nia adali kchiawwia.	I am the oldest.
Nia adali awôssiswia.	I am the youngest.
Awani paami kchiawwit kiuwô nisiwi?	Who is the oldest of you two?
Awani adali kchiawwit kiuwô nloiwi?	Who is the oldest of you three?
Nia.	It is I.
K'kasôbaiba?	How many brothers are you?
N'nisôbaibena, n'nesôbaibena, n'iawôbaibena.	We are two brothers, three, four brothers.
O'da n'wajônô (or n'wajônôw) nijia, or ôda n'owijiaiw.	I have no brother.
O'da 'waj'ônawi wijiaa, or ô'da wijiaiwi.	He has no brother.
O'da wajônawi widôbsoa, or ôda widôbsomiwi.	She has no brother; he has no sister.
Kasoak awôssisak k'wajônô?	How many children have you?
N'wajônô nguedôz awôssisak: nisoak wskinnosisak ta iawak nôkskuasisak.	I have six children: two boys and four girls. (*literally:* two little boys and four little girls).
Kasigadema adali kchiaowit k'-d-awôssisem?	How old is the oldest of your children? (your oldest child).

Adali kehiaowit n'-d-awôssisem nguedôz kasônkaw kasigadema.	The oldest of my children is sixteen years of age.
Kasigadema ato wa wski alnôba?	How old may this young man be?
Awôssisoo askua pita, kanwa kwenakuezo.	He is young yet, but he is tall.
Nadawiwi nikuôbi pmôwzowinino kwenôwzo nguedatgua.	It is seldom that a person now lives to the age of a hundred years
Nmahom nikwôbi nguedatguat taba iaw kasigadema.	My grandfather is now a hundred and four years of age.

(4. *On the hour*).

Kasômkipoda ato nekwôbi?	What o'clock may it be now?
Nguedômkipoda pabômiwi.	It is about one o'clock.
Tabenatta sôkhôban.	The daybreak will soon appear.
Kisos sôkhipozo.	The sun is rising.
Kizi nôwwat chakuat.	It is late (speaking in the morning).
O'da, askua pita spôzoo.	No, it is early yet (in the morning).
Tôni ato kwôbkisgad?	How late may it be (in the day)?
Kizi paskua.	It is already noon.
Kwaskuai paskua nikwôbi.	It is just noon now.
Môjob kizi paskuat nisômkipodak.	He started after twelve o'clock (noon)
Pagadosab nguedôz kasômkipodak spôzowiwi.	He came back at six o'clock in the morning.
Kizi nkihla.	It is sun down.
Kizi ato kamôjitebakad	It must be late in the night.
O'da, asma nôdamitebakadowi.	No, it is not yet late (in the night).
Kizi nôwitebakad?	Is it already midnight?
O'da, asmo nôwitebakadowi.	No, it is not yet midnight.
Kizi nikwôbi paami (*or* awasiwi) nôwitebakad.	It is now midnight past.
N'môjiji kizi nôwitebakka.	I will start after midnight.
Paiab nahnôwitebakka.	He (she) came at midnight.

K'ospôzi toki wigawôjiwi? (*sing.*) ⎱ K'ospôzi tokiba wigawôjiwi? (*plur.*) ⎰	Do you generally get up early in the morning?
N'ospôzi tokibenâ majimiwi.	We always get up early in the morning.
Chowi spôzi tokin majimiwi.	One must always get up early.
O'miki, (*or* ômki), nijia, kizi chakuat.	Get up, my brother, it is day light.
K'sazigôdam; k'ozômi sazipkekwsi.	You are lazy; you sleep too long.
Asma noliwi kasômkipodawi.	It is not yet nine o'clock.
Kina papisookuazik, kizi mdala kasômkipoda.	See the clock, it is already ten o'clock.
O'daaii môjowiwi papisookuazik.	That clock is not going.
O'da n'-d-aspiguôbakhamowenab.	I did not wind it up.
Tebaikisosôgan môjoo; kizi mdala taba pabasiwi.	The watch is going; it is now (already) half past ten.
Adoji ndup akuamadama, ôdaaba n'kizi ômikiw nikwôbi.	I have such a headache, I can't get up now.
Tôni w'toji nkihlôn (*or* nkosan) kisos nikwôbi?	At what time does the sun set?
Nkihla nguedôz taba pabasiwi.	It sets at half past six (o'clock).
Chiga k'môjiba wigiakw?	When will you go home?
Nmôjibenaji wigiak kwaskuai nônnômkipodaga.	We will go home at five o'clock precisely.
Tebaikisosôgan u (*or* u tebaikisosôgan) pita wligen.	This watch is very fine (*or* very good).
Wli tebaikisosôgan u.	This is a good watch.
Tôni llôwado?	How much did it cost?
Llôwado nisinska taba nôlan môniak.	It cost twenty five dollars.
Kizi u aawakamuk.	It is a second hand watch.
N'tebhikisosôgan wzômi kezosao.	My watch goes too fast.
Nia wzômi mannosao.	Mine goes too slow.
Agma wlosao.	His keeps the right time.
W'kiz'ônkohlôn w'tebhikisosôgan.	He has sold his watch.
N' kiz'ônkohlônana n'tebhibizosôganna.	We have sold our watch, (we, *you excluded*).
K'kiz'ônkohlônana k'tebhikizosôganna.	We have sold our watch, (we, *you included*).

(*5. On the weather*).

Tôni llekisgad.	How is the weather?
Wlekisgad.	It is fine weather.
O'da wlekisgadwi.	It is not fine weather.
Majkisgad.	It is bad weather.
Pita majkisgad, *or* pita neskekisgad.	The weather is very bad.
Asokwad?	Is it cloudy?
Asokwad.	It is cloudy.
Wli kakasakwad.	It is clear fair weather.
Kisosoo.	The sun shines.
O'da kisoswiwi.	The sun does not shine.
Pesgawan.	It is foggy.
Kzelômsenoso.	It blows a little.
Kinlômsen.	It blows hard, it is stormy.
Tkelômsen.	The wind blows cold.
Sakpôlômsen.	It blows a gale.
N'-d-elaldam soglônji pamekisgak.	I think it will rain today.
Soglônoso askua.	It rains a little yet.
Kizi akwlôn.	The rain is over.
Askua psôn.	It is snowing yet.
Soglônji mina pita nabiwi.	It will rain again very soon.
Noli wissebagezi.	I am all wet.
Nia achi n'wissebagezi.	I am wet too.
O'da kiuwô k'wissegezippa?	Are you not wet? (pl.)
Noli wissebagezibena.	We are all wet.
O'da n'wajônemoppena ôbagawatahigan.	We have no umbrella.
N'namihô managuôn.	I see the rainbow.
Idôza ni agua kadawi wawlekisgad.	They say that it is a sign of fine weather.
O'da majimiwi, wzômi nôngueji askua pepadlôn kôgasogueniwi.	Not always, because it sometimes rains for many days after.
Wawamamguat ali pilowelômsek.	One perceives that the wind is changed.
K'kinlônamibena walôguiga.	We had a great storm yesterday in the evening.
Tôni aiiakwza kwani padôgiiwik?	Where were you during the thunder storm.

N'-d-aib kikônek môja padôgiiwik.	I was in the field when it began to thunder.
K'nodam nawa kagui lli wagaloka padôgi?	Did you hear that the thunder has done any damage?
Padôgi pagessin aiamihawigamigok.	The thunder-bolt fell upon the church.
O'da awanihi nhlawi?	Did it kill anybody?
Asma wawalmeguadowi.	It is not known yet.
Pilaskwikokji chowi nodôguad.	The newspapers will not fail to give an account of it.
Melikaskadenji saba.	We shall have a hard frost tomorrow.
Kizi nikwôbi meliki keladen.	It freezes very hard now.
O'da môlhidahômguadowi: kwaskuai nikwôbi nôwi ppon.	It is not surprising: we are in the middle of winter.
N'kwaskuaji pita.	I am very cold.
Pidiga, nôdawazi.	Come in and warm your self.
Neljial ôbizmôgoowal.	My fingers are benumbed with cold.
Kamguena tkebik.	Steep them in cold water.
O'da n'-d-elaldamowenab ali tkebi wligek weji ni.	I didn't think that cold water was good for that.
Kizi kuinatta msôguata.	The snow is quite deep already.
Llaguinôguat pitaji mliki ppon pamikadek.	It is likely to be sharp this year.
Pita tkelômsem pami kizi paskuak.	The wind blows very cold this afternoon.

(6. On the time of the night).

Kizi adoji môjimuk, kizi kamôdlôguihla.	It is time to go, it grows late.
Kamôji k'wizaka, asma noliwi kasômkipodawi.	You are in a great hurry, it is not yet nine o'clock.
Noliwi? Kizi noliwi taba pabasiwi.	Nine (o'clock?) it is already half past nine.
Kagui wisakaman? asma nôdamitebakadowi.	What hurries you away so soon? it is not late, (speaking of the night).

Wzômiga n'kawi majiniwi mdala kasômkipodak.	It is because I usually go to bed at ten o'clock.
Adoji nadawiwi paiôan k'-d-achoiba paami sipkabi.	You come so seldom that you ought to stop a little longer.
Akuiga kagui llalda, n'pakaldamikhowab aliji pagadosaa asma mdala kasômkipodannokw.	You'll excuse me, (*lit:* be not offended,) I promised to be at home before ten o'clock.
N'-d-eli nkawatzi aliji saba paami sipkôdokaziakw.	I hope tomorrow we will be (talking) longer together.
Ni weji aiagaji paami nabi paiôana.	For that you will have to come earlier.
N'paiôji asma pezdannogw.	I'll be here before dark.
Adio.	Goodbye.

(7. *On arriving at the hotel*).

Nidôbak, u pita wlitebi nôguad sôghebaigamigw.	My friends, here is a respectable looking inn.
K'nawadosanana nawa u?	Shall we alight here?
Pidigada.	Let us go in.
N'kiziba tosgomenana u?	Can we stop over night here?
Pakalmeguat.	Of course.
K'wajônem nawa alômsagol sigwtagil?	Have you any spare rooms?
Kalaato, k'meznembaji walôjowigil alômsagwsisal ta abonal walikkil u tali.	Yes, gentlemen, you will find handsomely–furnished rooms and good beds here.
Lli wlalda k'olitebi ponsan, wzômi taketa nônôgajibena.	Please make a good fire, for we are benumbed with cold.
Azô, llosala ugik wdowinnoak kchi alômsagok, ni k'olitebi ponsan nitta.	John, show the gentlemen into the parlour, and make a good fire immediately.
Lli wlalda k'namitlin alômsagw tôni achowi tosgoma.	Please let me see the room I am to sleep in.
Mali, wdena wasanemôgan ni k'nôji namitlôn wa wdowinno w'-d-alômsagom.	Here, Mary, take a candle and show the gentleman to his room.

N'kiziba mzenem alômsagw ôwdik alagwtag?	Can I have a room looking into the street?
U adali wligek u tali wigwômek.	Sir, here is the best in the house.
K'-d-eli wlaldamenba k'tokimin nônômkipodaga spôsowiwi?	Would you (be so kind as to) awake me up at five o'clock in the morning?
Kalaato, ôdaaba n'wanaldamowen.	Yes, Sir[1], I will not forget it.

(8. To embark in a ship).

Nidôba, k'kiziba lhin tôni li ao u ktolagw alosaik Plachmônkik?	My friend, can you tell me if there is a ship in the harbour going to France?
N'-d-elaldam ao pazegwen.	I believe there is one.
K'kiziba lhin tôni li mojoo pamekisgak?	Can you tell me if she sails today?
N'-d-elaldam pamekisgak, kanwa waji pakaldaman, k'-d-achowiba klolô captin.	I believe she will; but to make sure, you must speak to the captain.
Tôni ait?	Where is he?
W'-d-alômsagomek.	In his office, (room).
Tôni aik w'-d-alômsagom, ala w'wigwôm?	Where is his office, or his house?
Captin ao (or wigo) kchi ôwdik, nônninska taba nôlan alagimguak, awasiwi post-office-ek.	The captain lives in the Main street, No 55, beyond the post-office.
Kizi w'-d-ain w'-d-office-mek.	He is in his office now.
Paakuinôgwzian, kaptin, chiga k'-d-elal-dam k'môjaaksi.	Good morning, captain, when do you expect to sail?
N'môjiji almitta ntami tamagak saba, wlitebelômsega.	I shall go by the first tide tomorrow, if the wind is favourable.
Kagui waji oda môjiwwan pamekisgak almittamina tamagak?	Why don't you go today by the next tide?

---

1. The term "Sir" or "Gentleman", expressed in Abenakis by Wdowinno, which means: man of high class, is always omitted in this language, when we address the person or persons themselves

Wzômiga w'-d-ainô kôgaswak pmôwsowinnoak kizi pakaldamikhogik aliba ôda môjiwwa nodôiwi saba; ta achi ôda maôwelômsenwi pamelôguik.

It is because I have several persons (passengers) to whom I have promised not to sail before tomorrow; and moreover the wind is not fair this evening.

Tôni llôwado alholdimuk?

What is the fare for the passage?

Nisinska taba nôlan môniak taba pabasiwi.

Twenty-five dollars and a half.

N'-d-ilhegaab ali wibiwi mdala.

I was told it was only ten.

Tôniji kweni pmakanninana sobagok?

How long shall we be at sea?

O'daaba n'kizi idamoweu kwaskuai, wzômi u akwôbigadek kzelômsen ôda pakalmeguadowi.

I can't tell exactly, because at the season the wind is uncertain.

(9. *On the point of leaving*).

Ni nikwôbi, nidôbak, k'kizi spôzipibena ta ôdabibena, ni k'-d-a chowi kistonana tôni k'-d-elkanninana li (*or* lli) *London*.

Now, my friends, we have had our breakfast and rested ourselves, we must decide which way we shall go to London.

Ao pegua kôgasnol ôwdial waji ni losamuk?

Are there several ways of going there?

O'hôô, k'kizi sasagosabena ta lli *London* stimbotek, ala k'pikagôbena lli *Dover* ni niwji alnahlagwôwdik lli *London*.

Yes, we can go direct to London by the steamer, or else cross to Dover, and thence to London by the railway.

Nadodemokada chiga môjahla stimbot.

Let us inquire when the steamboat starts.

N'-d-ilhega ali môjahlôg kwaskuai nônômkipodaga.

I am told that she leaves at five o'clock sharp.

Pitani wlitebosao kiuna wji; ni anegi nisômkipodak, k'wajônemebenaji kisokw waji pabômosaakw ta namitoagw odana.

That suits us very well; it is but two o'clock, we shall have time to walk (about) and see the city.

Kizi iawômkipoda mjessala nônônkaw, k'-d-achowi petegibena llaguiwi mamilitiganek.	It is a quarter to four, we must turn our steps towards the wharf.

(10. *On board the steamboat*).

Ni kizi k'pozinana.	Now we are on board.
K'nodamen *engine* altôguak?	Do you hear the noise of the engine?
O'da ni wibiwi, achi n'wawamadamen ali nanamipodak stimbot.	Not only that, but I also feel the steamboat shaking.
Kagui k'-d-elôwzi? K'pilwinôgwzi.	What is the matter with you? You look pale.
O'da n'olitebamalsiw; n'majilawôji paami sibkabiôna u wskidolagua.	I don't feel very well; I shall be seasick if I remain longer on deck.
Niga, losada kchi alômkagok.	Then, let us go in the main cabin.
Kizi k'-d-akuamalsi?	Are you sick already?
O'da (*or* ôdaagaki) taketa, kanwa pita n'majilawaamalsi.	Not exactly, but rather qualmish.
Niagaki wji, ôda kagui n'-d-iiliogowen sobagw.	As for me, I am not subject to seasickness.
Kizi n'mawiaamalsi. K'kiziji nikwôbi u ôainana, waji wlitebi namitoagw wigwômal tali *Dover*.	I feel better now. We can remain here now, so as to see distinctly the houses at Dover.
Tabenatta k'nôdagahlôbena; kizi pazôbin nôdagakik.	We shall soon arrive (land); we are in sight of land.

(11. *On Travelling by water in the Indian country*).

Nidôba chiga k'pozibena?	Friend, when shall we embark?
O'da n'wawaldomowen; ôdaaba alwa n'kizi môjiw pamalakamuk.	I don't know; I will probably not be able to start this week.
Kagui weji?	Why?
Wzômiga ôda n'odoliw.	Because I have no canoe.

K'kadawtoli nawa?	Do you intend to make a canoe?
Ohôô, n'olitqji pazegwen nabiwi; kizi n'wajônemen maskua.	Yes, I will make one soon; I have the bark already.
K'wajônô kôksk kasi chowalmôan?	Have you all the cedar you want?
Ohôô, n'wajônô.	Yes, I have.
K'nitôwtoli, nidôba.	You are skilful in making canoes, my friend.
Nôwatga n'noji tolin.	It is a long while since I have constantly made canoes.
Wlitawi nia achi pazegwen, nidôba; k'olôbankolji.	Make also one for me, my friend; I will pay you well.
K'olitolji pazegwen.	I will make you one.
U k'dol, nijia; k'mahôwinamen?	Here is your canoe, my brother; do you like it?
Kalaato, nidôba.	Certainly, friend.
Chowi ato melikigen.	I suppose it is strong.
U k'mônim.	Here is your money.
Wliwni, nijia, k'olitebi ôbankawi.	Thank you, brother, you pay me well.
K'pozibenaji Kissandaga, awibega.	We will embark Monday, if it is calm.
N'meskawô nisoak wski alnôbak waji wijawgoagw.	I have found two young fellows to come with us.
Ntôwibiak?	Are they good paddlers?
Mgeniganak, *or* mgeniganooak.	First rate.
O'da atoba paamadowi k'-d-ôdolibianana?	Would it not be better that we should row?
N'-d-elaldam wligenba; paami kesihlôn ôdolibiamuk ôdaki pamibiamuk.	I think it would be good; we go quicker by rowing, than by paddling.
Niga, kwilawaha ôdolibiôganak.	Well, look for the oars.
Haw, haw, nidôbak! Pozoldinaj! pita wlawiben.	Halloo, halloo, my friends! Let us embark! It is very calm.
Kaalatta wlawiben. Postoda meziwi k'-dahimnawal.	It is very calm indeed. Let us embark all our luggage.
Iaha, wskinnosisak, meliki ôdolibiagw.	Now, boys, row smartly.

Kakaswi kzelômsen; wlitebelomsen; sibakhahamôda.	There is more and more wind; the wind is fair; let us sail.
Enni! Kamôji k'ksaksibena.	Aha! We are sailing very fast.
Sam, wlitebokwaa; wli nsato senal.	Sam, steer well; look out for the rocks.
Kakaswi kinlômsen; kakaswi achi kinôtego.	It blows harder and harder; and the sea runs higher and higher.
Kaamôji! K'pozogobena.	Ah! The waves come in.
Ponagia sibakhigan.	Take down the sail.
Pitaji tabena sakpônôguat; nôdagakik llachowitoda, ala k'machinabena.	It will be dreadful; let us go towards the shore, lest we perish.
Sibo u ao pasojiwi?	Is there a river near?
Sibos u sôgdahla pasojiwi; niji aliphowaakw.	A small river comes in near here; we will fly there.
Ni llokuaa, Sam.	Steer for that place, Sam.
Ni k'polowanana.	Now we are out of danger.
Sakpônôguat! Kina nebes alinôguak!	A dreadful time! See, how the lake looks!
Kizillaji k'-d-ali sipki kezôdhogonana u.	We will perhaps be long wind-bound here.
Sibagtaamoda wôôbaksigamigw u tali, wskinnosisak, kadi soglôn; asokwad.	Let us pitch the tent here, boys, it will rain; it is cloudy.
Kizi soglôn.	It is raining now.
Pidigado k'-d-ahimnawal.	Bring in our luggage.
K'-d-achowi spôzi môjibena, wlekisgaka.	We must start early in morning, if it is fine weather.

12. *Usual conversation between two Indians, when they meet together in their hunting ground.*

Kuai! kuai!! Paakuinôgwzian, tôni k'-dollôwzin?	Halloo! Halloo!! I am glad to see you, how do you do?
N'wôwlôwzi, kia nawa tôni?	I am very well, and you?
N'wôwlôwzi nia achi, wliwni ni.	I am very well, thank you.
Tôni nawa k'-d-ôllalmegon?	What luck have you had?
N'olalmegwga pita pamalokamuk.	I have been very lucky this week.

N'pithô nisinska tmakuak ta nônnoak wnegigwak.	I have caught twenty beavers and five otters.
K'kelhô nawa mosbasak?	I Did you catch any minks?
N'kelhô nguedôz kasônkaw.	I have caught sixteen.
N'nihlô achi awasos.	I have also killed a bear.
Wikao?	Was he fat?
Kinigômo.	Very fat.
Kia nawa tôni k'-d-elalmegon?	And you, what luck have you had?
Tôni lligen k-d-aki? tmakuaika?	How is your ground? is there plenty of beaver?
O'da kuina; kanwa mozika.	Not much; but there is plenty of moose.
Kaswak nawa mozak k'nililô?	How many moose did you kill?
Nisinska taba nis.	Twenty-two.
Kamôji, pita ni wligen.	Well, that's very good.
K'pithô ato achi chowi wakaswak tmakuak.	You must have also caught few beavers.
O'hoo, n'pithô mdala.	Yes, I have caught ten.
Cha nikwôbi hli chiga k'kadi nahilô.	Now, tell me when you intend to go down.
N'-d-elaldam n'nahilôji kedak almalokamek.	I think I shall go down sometime next week.
N'wigiba nia achi kizôji ni tojiwi, waji nisi nahilôakw.	I wish I could get ready by that time, so as to go home with you.
Wigidahôdamanaga k'kasi nahilôn nia, k'-d-askawiholji tali Kwanôgamak.	If you like to come down with me, I will wait for you at Long Lake.
Niga wligen. Chaga chajabihlôda. Adio.	That's all right. Now let us part. Goodbye.
Adio, wli nanawalmezi.	Goodbye, take care of yourself.

EXAMPLES

Some blue ribbon,
Walôwigek silki, or:
Silki walôwigek.

I have some ribbon,
N'wajônem silki, or:
Silki n'wajônem.

Mary has some ribbon,
Mali wajônem silki, or:
Silki wajônem Mali,
Mali silki wajônem,
Silki Mali wajônem,
Wajônem silki Mali,
Wajônem Mali silki.

John has a gray hat,
Azô wajônem wibguigek asolkwôn, or:
Asolkwôn wibguigek wajônem Azô,
Wibguigek asolkwôn Azô wajônem,
Wajônem Azô wibguigek asolkwôn,
Azô wibguigek asolkwôn wajônem,
Wibguigek asolkwôn wajônem Azô,
Wajônem wibguigek Azô asolkwôn,
Asolkwôn wibguigek Azô wajônem.

OTHER EXAMPLES

SHOWING THE TRANSPOSITION OF THE AFFIXES
"JI" AND "BA."

I shall go to Montreal Sunday,
N'-d-elosaji Molian Sandaga, or:
Sandaga*ji* Molian n'-d-elosa,
Molian*ji* n'-d-elosa Sandaga,
Sandaga*ji* n'-d-elosa Molian,
Molian*ji* Sandaga n'-d-elosa,
N'-d-elosa*ji* Sandaga Molian.

I would go to New-York if I had money,
N'-d-elosaba New-York wajônemôshôna môni, or:
New-York*ba* * n'-d-closa wajônemôshôna môni,
Môni*ba* wajônemôshôna n'-d-elosa New-York,
N'-d-elosa*ba* New-York môni wajônemôshôna,
Môni*ba* wajônemôshôna New-York n'-d-elosa,
Wajônemôshôna*ba* môni n'-d-elosa New-York,
Wajônemôshôna*ba* môni New-York n'-d-elosa.

---

* As you see, the affixes *ji* and *ba*, the former denoting the *future*, and the latter, the *conditional*, are also transposed.

PART THIRD

The Parts of Speech

That May Be Conjugated.

1. CONJUGATION OF THE ANIMATE SUBSTANTIVE

(Nmitôgwes, father).

Present.—Singular.

Nmitôgwes.	My father.
Kmitôgwes.	Thy father.
Wmilôgwsa.	His (her) father.
Nmitôgwsena.	Our father, (*exclusive*).
Kmitôgwsena.	Our father, (*inclusive*).
Kmitôgwsowô.	Your father.
Wmitôgwsowô.	Their father.

Plural.

Nmitôgwsenawak.	Our fathers, (*excl.*)
Kmitôgwsowôk.	Your fathers.
Wmitôgwsowô.	Their fathers.

Past.—Singular.

Nmitôgwesega,	My late father,
Kmitôgwsenoga,	Our late father,
Kmitôgwsowôga,	Your late father.

Plural.

Nmitôgwsenogak,	Our late fathers,
Kmitôgwsowôgak,	Your late fathers,
Wmitôgwsowôga.	Their late fathers.

Nmitôgwesji...	My father will...
Kmitôgwesji...	Thy father will...
Wmitôgwsaji...	His father will...
Nmitôgwsenaji...	Our father will...
Kmitôgwsowôji...	Your father will...
Wmitôgwsowôji...	Their father will...

Plural.

Nmitôgwsenawakji...	Our fathers will...
Kmitôgwsowôkji...	Your fathers will...
Wmitôgwsowôji...	Their fathers will...

That is, their fathers respectively.

Conditional.—Present.

Nmitôgwesba...	My father would...
Kmitôgwesba...	Thy father would...
Wmitôgwsaba...	His father would...
Nmitôgwsenaba...	Our father would...
Kmitôgwsowôba.	Your father would...
Wmitôgwsowôba...	Their father would...

Plural.

Nmitôgwsenawakba...	Our fathers would...
Kmitôgwsowôkba...	Your fathers would...
Wmitôgwsowôba...	Their fathers would...

We conjugate likewise *nigawes*, my mother, *nmessis*, my sister, *etc.*, *etc.*

2. CONJUGATION OF THE ANIMATE SUBSTANTIVE.

(Kaoz, cow).

Present.—Singular.

N'kaozem.	My cow.
K'kaozem.	Thy cow.
W'kaozema.	His cow.
N'kaozemna.	Our cow.
K'kaozemwô.	Your cow.
W'kaozemwô.	Their cow.

Plural.

N'kaozemak.	My cows.
K'kaozemak.	Thy cows.
W'kaozema.	His cows.
N'kaozemnawak.	Our cows.
K'kaozemnôk.	Your cows.
W'kaozemwô.	Their cows.

Past.—Singular.

N'kaozemga.	The cow I had (*owned*).
N'kaozemnoga.	The cow we had (*owned*).

Plural.

N'kaozemgak.	The cows I h. (*owned*).
N'kaozemgak.	The cows we h. (*owned*)

Future.—Singular.

N'kaozemji ônkohlôn.	My cow will be sold.
W'kaozemaji ônkôhlôna	His cow will be sold.
N'kaozemnaji ônkôhlôn.	Our cow will be sold.
W'kaozemwôji ônkolôna.	Their cow will be sold.

N'kaozemakji ônkohôlnak,	My cows will be sold.
W'kaozemaji ônkohôhlôna,	His cows will be sold.
N'kaozemnawakji ônkohlônak,	Our cows will be sold.
W'kaozemwôji ônkohlôna.	Their cows will be sold.

Conditional.—Singular.

N'kaozemba ônkohlôn.	My cow would be sold
W'kaozemaba ônkohlôna.	His cow would be sold.
N'kaozemnaba ônkohlôn.	Our cow would be sold.
W'kaozemwôba ônkohlôna.	Their cow would be sold.

Plural.

N'kaozemakba ônkohlônak.	My cows would be sold.
W'kaozemaba ônkohlôna.	His cows would be sold.
N'kaozemnawakba ônkohlônak.	Our cows would be sold.
W'kaozemwôba ônkôhlôna.	Their cows would be sold.

We conjugate likewise *n'-d-aasom*, my horse, *n'-d-aksenem*, my ox, *etc., etc.*

3. CONJUGATION OF THE ANIMATE SUBSTANTIVE.

(Alemos, dog).

Present.—Singular.

N'-d-amis.	My dog.
K'-d-amis,	Thy dog.
W'-d-amisa.	His dog.
N'-d-amisna.	Our dog.
K'-d-amiswô.	Your dog.
W'-d-amiswô.	Their dog.

Plural.

N'-d-amisak.	My dogs.
K'-d-amisak.	Thy dogs.
W'-d-amisa.	His dogs.
N'-d-amisnawak.	Our dogs.
K'-d-amiswôk.	Your dogs.
W'-d-amiswô.	Their dogs.

Past.—Singular.

N'-d-amisga,	The dog I had.
N'-d-amisnoga,	The dog we had.

Plural.

N'-d-amisnogak,	The dogs we had.
W'-d-amiswôga,	The dogs they had.

Future.—Singular.

N'-d-amisji k'sagamegw	My dog will bite thee.
W'-d-amisaji etc.	His dog will etc.
N'-d-amisnaji etc.	Our dog will etc.
W'-d-amiswôji etc.	Their dog will etc.

Plural.

N'-d-amisakji k'sagamegok.	My dogs will bite thee.
W'-d-amisaji k'sagamegok.	His dogs will bite thee.
N'-d-amisnawakji k'sagamegok.	Our dogs will bite thee.
W'-d-amiswôji k'sagamegok.	Their dogs will bite thee.

Conditional.—Singular.

N'-d-amisba w'sagamô.	My dog would bite him.
W'-d-amisaba etc.	His dog would bite him.
N'-d-amisnaba etc.	Our dog would bite him.
W'-d-amiswôba etc.	Their dog would bite him.

N'-d-amisakba w'sagamôwô.	My dogs would bite them.
W'-d-amisaba w'sagamôwô.	His dogs would bite them.
N'-d-amisnawakba w'sagamôwô.	Our dogs would bite them.
W'-d-amiswôba w'sagamôwô.	Their dogs would bite them.

4. CONJUGATION OF THE INANIMATE SUBSTANTIVE.

(Paskhigan, gun).

Present.—Singular.

N'paskhigan.	My gun.
K'paskhigan.	Thy gun.
W'paskhigan.	His gun.
N'paskhiganna.	Our gun.
K'paskiganowô.	Your gun.
W'paskhiganowô.	Their gun.

Plural.

N'paskhiganal.	My guns.
K'paskhiganal.	Thy guns.
W'paskhiganal.	His guns.
N'paskhigannawal.	Our guns.
K'paskihiganowôl.	Your guns.
W'paskhiganowôl.	Their guns.

Past.—Singular.

N'paskhigana.	The gun I had (*owned*).
N'paskhigannawa.	The gun we had (*owned*).

Plural.

N'paskhiganegal.	The guns I had (*owned*).
N'paskhigannogal.	The guns we had (*owned*).

Future.—Singular.

N'paskhiganji ônkohlôn	My gun will be sold.
N'paskhigannaji etc.	Our gun will be sold.
K'paskhiganowôji etc.	Your gun will be sold.

Plural.

N'paskhiganalji ônkohlônal.	My guns will be sold.
N'paskhigannawalji etc	Our guns will be sold.
W'paskhiganowôlji etc.	Their guns will be sold.

Conditional.—Singular.

N'paskhiganba ônkohlôn.	My gun would be sold
N'paskhigannaba etc.	Our gun would be etc.
W'paskhiganowôba etc.	Their gun would be etc.

Plural.

N'paskhiganalba ônkohlônal.	My guns would be sold.
N'paskhigannawalba.	Our guns would be etc.
W'pasbhigannawôlba	Their guns would be etc.

THE FOREGOING CONJUGATION,

N'kaozem, my cow, transformed into *possessive* verb: *Okaozemimuk*, to have a cow.

INDICATIVE MOOD.

Present.

N'okaozemi.	I have a cow.
'okaozemo.	He has a cow.
N'okaozemibena	We have a cow.
K'okaozemiba.	You have a cow.
'Okaozemoak.	They have a cow.

Imperfect.

N'okaozemib.	I had a cow.
'Okaozemob.	He had a cow.
N'okaozemibenob.	We had a cow.
K'okaozemibôb.	You had a cow.
'Okaozemobanik.	They had a cow.

Future.

N'okaozemiji.	I shall have a cow.
'Okaozemoji.	He will have a cow.
N'okaozemibenaji.	We shall have a cow.
K'okaozemibaji.	You will have a cow.
'Okaozemoakji.	They will have a cow.

Second Future.

N'okaozemiji kizi, or, Kiziji n'okaozemi.	I shall have had a cow.
'Okaozemoji kizi.	He will have had a cow.
'Okaozemoakji kizi.	They will have had a cow.

CONDITIONAL MOOD.

Present.

N'okaozemiba.	I should have a cow.
'Okaozemoba.	He would have a cow.
N'okaozemibenaba.	We should have a cow.
'Okaozemoakba.	They would have a cow.

Past.

N'okaozemibba.	I should have had a cow.
'Okaozemobba.	He would have had etc.
N'okaozemibenobba.	We should have had etc.
'Okaozemobanikba.	They would have had etc.

IMPERATIVE MOOD.

Okaozemi.	Have a cow.
Okaozemij.	Let him have a cow.
Okaozemida.	Let us have a cow.
Okaozemigw.	Have a cow.
Okaozemidij.	Let them have a cow.

SUBJUNCTIVE MOOD.

Present.

N'okaozemin.	That I may have a cow.
'Okaozemin.	That he may have a cow.
N'okaozeminana.	That we may have a cow.
K'okaozeminô.	That you may have a cow.
'Okaozeminô.	That they may have a cow.

Past.

Kizi n'okaozemin.	That I might have had a cow.

etc., after the above tense, commencing by *kizi*.

Imperfect.

N'okaozeminaza.	That I might have a cow.
'Okaozeminaza.	That he might have a cow.
N'okaozeminanossa.	That we might have a cow.
K'okaozeminôssa	That you might have a cow.
'Okaozeminôssa.	That they might have a cow.

Pluperfect.

Kizi n'okaozeminaza.	That I might have had a cow.

etc., after the *Imperfect*, commencing by *kisi*.

CONJUGATION OF THE ADJECTIVE-VERB

Wôbigimuk, to be white.

INDICATIVE MOOD.

Present.

N'wôbigi.	I am white.
K'wôbigi.	Thou art white.
'Wôbigo.	He (she) is white.
N'wôbigibena.	We are white. (*excl.*)
K'wôbigibena.	We are white. (*incl.*)
K'wôbigiba.	You are white.
'Wôbigoak.	They are white.

Imperfect.

N'wôbigib.	I was white.
K'wôbigib.	Thou wast white.
Wôbigob.	He was white.
N'wôbigibenob.	We were white.
K'wôbigibôb.	You were white.
'Wôbigobanik.	They were white.

Future.

N'wôbigiji.	I shall be white.

etc., after the above *present tense*, affixing *ji*, to the verb.

Second Future.

N'wôbigiji kizi, or:	I shall have been white.
Kiziji n'wokigi, etc.	etc., etc.

Conditional Mood.

Present.

N'wôbigiba. | I should be white.
   etc., after the *present tense*, affixing *ba* to the verb.

Past.

N'wôbigibba. | I should have been white.
   etc., after the *imperfect tense*, affixing *ba* to the verb.

Imperative.

Wôbigi.	Be white.
Wôbigij.	Let him be white.
Wôbigej.	*Let it be white.*
Wôbigida.	Let us be white.
Wôbigigw.	Be white.
Wôbigiidij.	Let them be white.
Wôbigej.	*Let them be white, (things).*

Subjunctive Mood.

Present.

N'wôbigin. etc., etc.	That I may be white. etc., etc.
N'wôbiginana.	That we may be white.
K'wôbiginô.	That you may be white.
W'wôbiginô.	That they may be white.

Past.

Kizi n'wôbigin. | That I may have been white.
   etc., after the immediately *preceding* tense, commencing by *kizi*.

Imperfect.

N'wôbiginaza. etc., etc.	That I might be white. etc., etc.
N'wôbiginanossa.	That we might be white.
K'wôbiginôssa.	That you might be white.
W'wôbiginôssa.	That they might be white.

Pluperfect.

Kizi n'wôbiginaza.	That I might have been white.

etc., after the *imperfect* tense, commencing always by *kizi.*

NEGATIVE CONJUGATION

Of the foregoing possessive verb "okaoze-mimuk."

INDICATIVE MOOD.

Present.

O'da n'okaozemiw.	I have no cow.
" 'okaozemiwi.	He has no cow.
" n'okaozemippena.	We have no cow.
" k'okaozemippa.	You have no cow.
" 'okaozemiwiak.	They have no cow.

Imperfect.

O'da n'okaozemib.	I had no cow.
" 'okaozemiwib.	He had no cow.
" n'okaozemippenop.	We had no cow.
" k'okaozemippôp.	You had no cow.
" 'okaozemi wibanik.	They had no cow.

Past definite.

O'da n'okamiibozemiib.	I had no cow.
" 'okaozemiwi.	He had no cow.
" n'okaozemippenoop.	We had no cow.

O'da k'okaozemippôôp.	You had no cow.
" 'okaozemiwibanik.	They had no cow.

Future.

Odaaba n'okaozemiw.	I shall have no cow.

etc., as in the *present tense*, commencing always by *o'daaba.*

Second future.

Asmaji n'okaozemiw.	I shall have had no cow

etc., also as in the *present tense*, always commencing by *asmaji.*

Conditional Mood.

Present.

O'daaba n'okaozemiw.	I should have no cow.

etc., as in the *future tense.*

Past.

O'daaba n'okaozemib.	I should h. had no cow.

etc., as in the *imperfect tense*, commencing by *ôdaaba.*

Imperative Mood.

Akui 'okaozemi.	Have no cow.
" 'okaozemij.	Let him have no cow.
" 'okaozemida.	Let us have no cow.
" 'okaozemikagw.	Have no cow.
" 'okaozemiidij.	Let them have no cow.

Subjunctive Mood.

Present.

O'da n'okaozemiwwen.	That I may have no cow.
" 'okaozemiwwen.	That he may have no cow.
" n'okaozemiwnana.	That we may have no cow.

O'da k'okaozemiwnô.	That you may have no cow.
" 'okaozemiwnô.	That they may have no cow.

Imperfect.

O'da n'okaozemiwnaza.	That I might have no cow.
O'da 'okaozemiwnaza	That he might have no cow.
O'da n'okaozemiwnanossa.	That we might have no cow.
O'da k'okaozemiwnôssa.	That you might have no cow.
O'da 'okaozemiwnôssa.	That they might have no cow.

This *tense* is used also for the *past* and the *pluperfect* tenses.

AFFIRMATIVE CONJUGATION

Of the *animate* objective verb, *wajônômuk*, to have.

(*Indefinite conjugation*).

Indicative Mood.

Present.

N'wajôno ases.	I have a horse.
K'wajônô etc.	Thou hast etc.
'Wajôna.*	He (she) has etc.
N'wajônôbena ⎫ etc. K'wajônôbena ⎭	We have etc.
K'wajônôba etc.	You have etc.
'Wajônak.*	They have etc.

Imperfect.

N'wajônôb kaoz.	I had a cow.
K'wajônôb etc.	Thou hadst etc.
'Wajônab.*	He had etc.
N'wajônôbenob etc. ⎫ K'wajônôbenob etc. ⎭	We had etc.

---

* Say: 'Wajôna, 'wajônak, *asessa;* 'wajônab, 'wajônabanik, *kaoza;*——, *aziba.*

| K'wajônôbôb etc. | You had etc. |
| 'Wajônabanik. * | They had etc. |

Past definite.

N'wajônôôb azib.	I had a sheep.
K'wajônôôb.	Thou hadst etc.
'Wajônab. *	He had etc.
N'wajônôbenoob ⎫ K'wajônôbenoob ⎭	We had etc.
K'wajônôbôôb.	You had etc.
'Wajônabanik. *	They had etc.

The *past definite* tense is used also for the *past indefinite* and *pluperfect* tenses.

Future

N'wajônôji alemos.	I shall have a dog.
K'wajônoji etc.	Thou wilt have etc.
'Wajônaji *	He will have etc.
N'wajônôbenaji ⎫ K'wajônôbenaji ⎭ etc.	We shall have.
K'wajônôbaji etc.	You will have etc.
Wajônakji. *	They will have etc.

Second Future.

| N'wajônôji kizi. | I shall have had. |

etc., as above, putting always *kizi* after the verb.

CONDITIONAL MOOD.

Present.

N'wajônôba asesak.	I should have some horses.
K'wajônôba etc.	Thou wouldst have etc.
'Wajônaba. *	He would have etc.

---

* Say: 'Wajônaji, wajônakji, *alemossa;* 'wajônaba, 'wajô-nakba, *asessa.*

N'wajônôbenaba ⎫ etc. K'wajônôbenaba ⎭	We should have etc.
K'wajônôbaba etc.	You would have etc.
Wajônakba.*	They would have etc.

Past.

N'wajônôbba kaozak.	I should have had some cows.
K'wajônôbba etc.	Thou wouldst have had etc.
'Wajônabba.*	He would have had etc.
N'wajônôbenobba ⎫ etc. K'wajônôbenobba ⎭	We should have had etc
K'wajônôbôbba etc.	You would have had etc.
Wajônabanikba.†	They would have had etc.

IMPERATIVE MOOD.

Wajôna.	Have (thou.)
Wajônôj.	Let him have.
Wajônôda.	Let us have.
Wajônogw.	Have (ye or you).
Wajônôôdij.	Let them have.

SUBJUNCTIVE MOOD.

Present.

N'wajônôn azibak.	That I may have some sheep.
K'wajônen etc.	That thou mayest have
W'wajônôn.*	That he may have etc.
N'wajônônana ⎫ etc. K'wajônônana ⎭	That we may have etc.
K'wajônônô etc.	That you may have etc.
W'wajônônô.*	That they may have etc.

---

* Here, say: Wajônabba, wajônabanikba, *kaoza.*

† Say: W'wajônôn, w'wajônônô, *aziba.*

N'wajônônaza.	That I might have.
K'wajônônaza.	That thou mightst have
W'wajônônaza.	That he might have.
N'wajônônanossa. ⎫ etc.	That we might have.
K'wajônônanossa. ⎭	
K'wajônônôssa.	That you might have.
W'wajônônôssa.	That they might have.

Past.

Kizi n'wajônôn, *or* n'wajônôn kizi.	That I may have had.

etc., as in the above *present tense*, putting always *kizi* before the pronoun, or after the verb.

Pluperfect.

Kizi n'wajônônaza or n'wajônônaza kizi.	That I might have had.

etc., as in the above *imperfect tense*, putting always *kizi* before the pronoun, or after the verb.

AFFIRMATIVE CONJUGATION

Of the *animate* objective verb, *wajônômuk*, to have.

(Finite Conjugation).

INDICATIVE MOOD.

Present.

N'wajônô ases.	I have the horse.
K'wajônô etc.	Thou hast etc.
W'wajônô *	He has the horse.

---

* Here, we say: W'wajônô, w'wajônôwô, *asessa;* w'wajônôbani, w'wajônôwôbani, *kaoza.*

N'wajônônna ⎫ tases	
K'wajônônna ⎭	We have etc.
K'wajônôwô etc.	You have etc.
W'wajônôwô *	They have etc.

Imperfect.

N'wajônôb kaoz.	I had the cow.
W'wajônôbani *	He had etc.
N'wajônônnôb etc.	We had etc.
K'wajônôwôb etc.	You had etc.
W'wajônôwôbani *	They had etc.

This tense is used also for the *past definite*, the *indefinite* and the *pluperfect* tenses.

Future.

N'wajônôji.	I shall have.

etc., after the *present* tense, affixing *ji* to the verb.

Second Future.

N'wajônôji kizi.	I shall have had.

etc., as in the simple *future* tense, ending by *kizi*.

CONDITIONAL MOOD.

Present.

N'wajônôba alemos.	I should have the dog.
W'wajônôba †	He would have etc.
N'wajônônnaba etc.	We should have etc.
K'wajônôwôba etc.	You would have etc.
W'wajônôwôba †	They would have etc.

---

* Here, we say: W'wajônô, w'wajônôwô, *asessa;* w'wajônôbani, w'wajônôwôbani, *kaoza*.
† W'wajônôba, w'wajônôwôba, *alemossa*

N'wajônôbba nolka.	I should have had the deer.
W'wajônôbaniba etc.	He would have had etc.
N'wajônônobba etc.	We should have had etc.
K'wajônôwabba etc.	You would have had etc.
W' wajônôwôbaniba &.	They would have had etc.

The remaining *moods* and *tenses* are to be conjugated as in the foregoing *indefinite* conjugation.

AFFIRMATIVE CONJUGATION

Of the *inanimate* objective verb, *wajônôzik* to have.

(*Indefinite conjugation*).

INDICATIVE MOOD

Present.

N'wajônem awighigan.	I have a book.
K'wajônem etc.	Thou hast etc.
'wajônem etc. N'wajônemebena etc. }	He has etc.
K'wajônemebena etc.	We have etc.
K'wajônemeba etc.	You have etc.
'wajônemok etc.	They have etc.

Imperfect.

N'wajônemob pilaskw.	I had some paper.
K'wajônemob etc.	Thou hadst etc.
'wajônemob etc.	He had etc.
N'wajônemebenob etc.	We had etc.
K'wajônemebôb etc.	You had etc.
'wajônemobanik etc.	They had etc.

Past definite.

N'wajônemoob paks.	I had a box.
K'wajônemoob etc.	Thou hadst etc.
'wajônemob etc.	He had etc.
N'wajônemebenoob etc.	We had etc.
K'wajônemebôôb etc.	You had etc.
'wajônemobanik etc.	They had etc.

This tense is also used for the *indefinite past* and the *pluperfect* tenses.

Future.

N'wajônemji.	I shall have.

etc., as in the *present tense*, always affixing *ji* to the verb.

Second Future.

N'wajônemji kizi.	I shall have had.

etc., as above, ending always by *kizi*.

CONDITIONNAL MOOD.

Present.

N'wajônemba môni.	I should have some money.
K'wajônemba etc.	Thou wouldst have etc.
'Wajônemba etc.	He would have etc.
N'wajônemebenaba etc.	We should have etc.
K'wajônemebaba etc.	You would have etc.
'Wajônemokba etc.	They would have etc.

Past.

N'wajônemobba mijo-wôgan.	I should have had some provisions.
K'wajônemobba etc.	Thou wouldst have had etc.
'Wajônemobba etc.	He would have had etc.
N'wajônemebenobba etc.	We should have had etc.

K'wajônemebôbba etc.	You would have had etc.
Wajônemobanikba etc.	They would have had etc.

IMPERATIVE MOOD.

Wajôna.	Have (thou).
Wajônej.	Let him have.
Wajônemoda.	Let us have.
Wajônemogw.	Have (ye or you).
Wajônemoodij.	Let them have.

SUBJUNCTIVE MOOD.

Present.

N'wajônemen. [a]	That I may have.
W'wajônemen.	That he may have.
N'wajônemenana.	That we may have.
K'wajônemenô.	That you may have.
W'wajenômenô.	That they may have.

Imperfect.

N'wajônemenaza. [b]	That I might have.
W'wajônemenaza.	That he might have.
N'wajônemenanossa.	That we might have.
K'wajônemenôssa.	That you might have.
W'wajônemenôssa.	That they might have.

Past.

Kizi n'wajônemen. [c]	That I may have had.

etc., as in the *present*, commencing by *kizi*.

---

a. NOTE.—*N'wajônemen*, etc. means also: I have it, etc.

b. N'wajonemenaza, etc means equally: I see (I find out) that I had it, etc.

c. Kizi n'wajônemen, I have it already.

Kizi n'wajônemenaza. | That I might have had.
    etc., after the *imperfect*, commencing by *kizi*.

AFFIRMATIVE CONJUGATION

Of the *inanimate* objective verb, *wajônôzik*, to have.

[*Finite Conjugation.*]

INDICATIVE MOOD.

Present.

N'wajônemen		I have the book.
K'wajônemen		Thou hast etc.
W'wajônemen	awighigan.	He has etc.
N'wajônemenana }		We have etc.
K'wajônemenana }		
K'wajônemenô		You have etc.
W'wajônemenô		They have etc.

Imperfect.

N'wajônemenab		I had the paper.
W'wajônemab		He had etc.
N'wajônemenanob	pilaskw.	We had etc.
K'wajônemenôb		You had etc.
W'wajônemenô		They had etc.

Future.

N'wajônemenji. | I shall have.
    etc., as above after the *present* tense, affixing always *ji* to the verb.

N'wajônemenji kizi.	I shall *or* will have had.

etc., as in the *simple future*, ending by *kizi*.

CONDITIONAL MOOD.

Present.

N'wajônemenba môni.	I should have the money.
K'wajônemenba etc.	Thou wouldst have etc.
W'wajônemenba etc.	He would have etc.
N'wajônemenanaba etc.	We should have etc.
K'wajônemenôba etc.	You would have etc.
W'wajônemenôba etc.	They would have etc.

Past.

N'wajônemenabba paskhigan.	I should have had the gun.
K'wajônemenabba etc.	Thou wouldst have had etc.
W'wajônemenabba etc.	He would have had etc.
N'wajônemenanôbba etc	We should have had etc.
K'wajônemenôbba etc.	You would have had etc
W'wajônemenôbba etc.	They would have had etc.

The remaining *moods* and *tenses* are to be conjugated as in the *indefinitive* conjugation.

NEGATIVE CONJUGATION

Of the *indefinite* verb, *wajônômuk*, to have.

INDICATIVE MOOD.

Present.

O'da n'wajônôw namas.	I have no fish.
" 'wajônawi *	He has no etc.

---

* Say: ôda 'wajônawi *namasa.*

O'da n'wajônôppena etc.	We have no etc.
" k'wajônôppa etc.	You have no etc.
" 'wajônawiak *	They have no etc.

Imperfect.

O'da 'wajônôb nolka.	I had no deer.
" 'wajônawib etc.	He had no etc.
" n'wajônôppenop etc.	We had no etc.
O'da k'wajônôppôp etc. ka.	You had no etc.
" 'wajônawibanik etc.	They had no etc.

This tense is used also for the *past definite*, the *indefinite* and the *pluperfect* tenses.

Future.

O'daaba n'wajônôw tmakwa.	I shall have no beaver.
O'daaba 'wajônawi etc.	He will have no etc.
O'daaba n'wajônôppena etc.	We shall have no etc.
O'daaba k'wajônôppa etc.	You will have no etc.
O'daaba 'wajônawiak etc.	They will have no etc.

Second Future.

Asmaji n'wajônôw.	I shall not have had.
" 'wajônawi.	He will not have had.
" 'wajônawiak.	They will not have had

Conditional Mood.

Present.

O'daaba n'wajônôb.	I should have no.
" 'wajônawib.	He would have no
" 'wajônawibanik	They would have no.

Past.

Asmaba n'wajônôw.	I should not have had.

"	'wajônawi.	He would not have had.
"	'wajonawiak.	They would not have had

IMPERATIVE MOOD.

Akui wajôna.	Have no.
" wajônôkij.	Let him have no.
" wajônôda.	Let us have no.
" wajônogw.	Have no.
" wajônôôdikij.	Let them have no.

SUBJUNCTIVE MOOD.

Present.

O'da n'wajônôwen.	That I may not have.
" n'wajônôwnana.	That we may not have.
" k'wajônôwnô.	That you may not have.

Imperfect.

O'da n'wajônôwnaza.	That I might not have.
" n'wajônêwnanossa.	That we might not have.
" k'wajônôwnôssa.	That you might not have.

Past.

Asma n'wajônôwen.	That I may not have had.
" n'wajônôwnana.	That we may not have had.
" k'wajônôwnô.	That you may not have had.

Pluperfect.

Asma n'wajônôwnaza.	That I might not have had.
" n'wajônôwnanossa.	That we might not have had.
" k'wajônôwnossa.	That you might not have had.

NEGATIVE CONJUGATION

Of the *finite* verb *wajônômuk, to have.*

INDICATIVE MOOD.

Present.

O'da n'wajônôwi ases.	I have not the horse.
" k'wajônôwi etc.	Thou hast not etc.
" w'wajônôwia *	He has not etc.
" n'wajônôwinna etc	We have not etc
" k'wajônôwiwwô etc	You have not etc.
" w'wajônôwiwwô.*	They have not etc.

Imperfect.

O'da n'wajônôwib kaoz.	I had not the cow.
O'da w'wajônôwibani †	He had not etc.
O'da n'wajônôwinnob koaz.	We had not the cow.
O'da k'wajônôwiwwôb etc.	You had not etc.
O'da w'wajônewiwwôbani. †	They had not etc.

This tense is also used for the *past definite*, the *indefinite*, and the *pluperfect* tenses.

Future.

O'daaba n'wajônôwi.	I shall not have.

etc., as above in the *present* tense, always commencing by *ôdaaba.*

Second Future.

Asmaji n'wajônôwi.	I will not have had.

etc., after the *preceding* tense, commencing always by *asemaji* instead of *ôdaaba.*

---

* Say:—W'wajônôwia, w'wajônôwiwwô, *asessa;*—w'wajônôwibani *kaoza.*
† Say:—w'wajônôwôwibani *kaoza.*

Conditional Mood.

Present.

O'daaba n'wajônôwi.	I should not have.
" w'wajônôwia.	He would not have.
" n'wajônôwinna.	We would not have.
" w'wajônôwiwô.	You would not have.

etc., as in the *present* tense, commencing always by *ôdaabo.*

Past.

O'daaba n'wajônôwib.	I should not have had.
" w'wajônôwibani.	He would not have had.
" n'wajônôwinnop.	We should not have had.

etc., as in the *imperfect* tense, commencing always by *ôdaaba.*

The remaining *moods* and *tenses* are to be conjugated as in the *indefinite* conjugation.

NEGATIVE CONJUGATION

Of the *indefinite* verb, *wajônôzik,* to have.

Indicative Mood.

Present.

O'da n'wajônemo awighiganebi.	I have no ink.
O'da k'wajônemo etc.	Thou hast no etc.
O'da 'wajônemowi etc.	He has no etc.
O'da n'wajônemoppena etc.	We have no etc.
O'da k'wajônemoppa etc.	You have no etc.
O'da 'wajônemowiak etc.	They have no etc.

Imperfect.

O'da n'wajônemob moswa.	I had no handkerchief.
O'da k'wajônemob etc.	Thou hadst no etc.
O'da 'wajônemowib moswa.	He had no handkerchief.

O'da n'wajônemoppenop etc.	We had no etc.
O'da k'wajônemoppôp etc.	You had no etc.
O'da 'wajônemowibanik etc.	They had no etc.

Future.

Odaaba n'wajônemo.	I shall have no.

etc., after the *present* tense, commencing by *ôdaaba.*

Second Future.

Asmaji n'wajônemo.	I shall not have had.

etc., after the *present* tense, commencing always by *asmaji.*

Conditional Mood.

Present.

O'daaba n'wajônemo.	I should have no.

etc., as in the *future* tense.

Past.

O'daaba n'wajônemob.	I should not have had.

etc., after the *imperfect* tense, commencing always by *ôdaaba.*

Imperative Mood.

Akui wajôna.	Have no.
" wajônej.	Let him have no.
" wajônemoda.	Let us have no.
" wajônemogw.	Have no.
" wajônemoodij.	Let them have no.

Subjunctive Mood.

Present.

O'da n'wajônemowen. *	That I may not have.
" w'wajônemowen.	That he may not have.
" n'wajônemownana.	That we may not have.
" k'wajônemownô.	That you may not have.
" w'wajônemownô.	That they may not have.

Imperfect.

O'da n'wajônemow-naza.	That I might not have.
" w'wajônemow-naza.	That he might not have.
" n'wajônemow-nanôssa.	That we might not have.
" k'wajônemow-nôssa.	That you might not have.
" w'wajônemow-nôssa.	That they might not have.

Past.

Asma n'wajônemowen.†	That I may not have had.

Pluperfect.

Asma n'wajônemownaza.	That I might not have had.

etc., as above in the *imperfect* tense, commencing always by *asma*.

NEGATIVE CONJUGATION

Of the *finite* verb, *wajônôzik*, to have.

Indicative Mood.

Present.

O'da n'wajônemowen ôbagawataigan.	I have not the umbrella.
O'da w'wajônemowen etc.	He has not etc.

---

* *O'da n'wajonemowen* means also: *I have it not.*
† *Asma n'wajonemowen,* I have it not yet.

O'da n'wajônemownana etc.	We have not etc.
O'da k'wajônemownô etc.	You have not etc.
O'da n'wajônemownô etc.	They have not etc.

Imperfect.

O'da n'wajônemowenab ôbadahon.	I had not the cane.
O'da w'wajônemowenab etc.	He had not etc.
O'da n'wajônemownanop etc.	We had not etc.
O'da kwajônemownôp etc.	You had not etc.
O'da w'wajônemownôp etc.	They had not etc.

Future.

O'daaba n'wajônemowen, sakhiljahon.	I shall not have the ring.

etc., after the *present* tense, commencing by *ôdaaba.*

Second Future.

Asmaji n'wajônemowen.	I shall not have had.

etc., after the *present* tense, commencing always by *asmaji.*

CONDITIONAL MOOD.

Present.

O'daaba n'wajônemowen.	I should not have.

etc., as in the *future* tense.

Past.

O'daaba n'wajônemowenab.	I should not have had.

etc., after the *imperfect* tense, commencing by *ôdaaba.*

The remaining *moods* and *tenses* are to be conjugated as in the *immediately* preceding conjugation.

DUBITATIVE CONJUGATION

Of the *animate* verb, *wajônômuk*, to have (*Literal*).

INDICATIVE MOOD.

Present.

Wskebi wajônok telaps. *	Perhaps I have a trap.
Wskebi wajônôan etc.	" thou hast etc.
" wajônôd. †	" he has etc.
" wajônôak etc.	" we have etc.
" wajônôakw etc.	" you have etc.
" wajônôôdit. †	" they have etc.

Imperfect.

Wskebi wajônokza tôbi. *	Perhaps I had a bow.
Wskebi wajônôaza etc.	" thou hadst etc.
" wajônôza etc. †	" he had etc.
" wajônôakza etc.	" we had etc.
" wajônôakwza etc.	" you had etc.
Wskebi wajônôôdiza †	" they had etc.

This tense is also used for the *past indefinite* and the *pluperfect* tenses.

Future.

Wskebiji wajônok.	Perhaps I will have.

etc., as in the *present* tense, placing always *wskebiji* before the verb.

Second Future.

Wskebiji kizi wajônok	Perhaps I will have have.

etc. after the *simple future*, putting *wskebiji kizi* before the verb.

---

* Always remember that the *personified* things, being always treated as if they were *animate*, go and agree with the *animate* verbs.

† Say: wajônôd, w'ajônôôdit *telapsa;* wajônôza, wajônôôdiza, *tôbia.*

Conditional Mood.

Present.

Wskebiba wajônok.	Perhaps I would have.

etc., after the *imperfect* tense, commencing by *wskebiba*.

Subjunctive Mood.

Present.

Wskebiji wajônoga.	Perhaps if I have.
" wajônôana.	" if thou hast.
" wajônôda.	" if he has.
" wajônôaga.	" if we have.
" wajônôagua.	" if you have.
" wajônôôdida.	" if they have.

Imperfect.

Wskebiba wajônogeshana.	Perhaps if I had.
Wskebiba wajônôashana.	" if thou hadst.
Wskebiba wajônôshana.	" if he had.
Wskebiba wajônôageshana.	Perhaps if we had.
Wskebiba wajônoa-gueshana.	" if you had.
Wskebiba wajônôôdishana.	" if they had.

DUBITATIVE CONJUGATION.

Of the *inanimate* verb, *wajônôzik*, to have.

(*Literal*).

Indicative Mood.

Present.

Wskebi wajônema môni	Perhaps I have some money.
" wajôneman etc.	" thou hast etc.

Wskebi wajônek etc.	Perhaps he has etc.
" wajônemag etc.	" we have etc.
" wajônemagw	" You have c&.
" wajônemoodit etc.	" They have etc.

Imperfect.

Wskebi wajô nemôza wizôwimôni.	Perhaps I had some gold.
Wskebi wajônemaza etc.	" thou hadst etc.
Wskebi wajônekeza etc.	" he had etc.
Wskebi wajônemakza etc.	" we had etc.
Wskebi wajônemakwza wizôwimôni.	Perhaps you had some gold.
Wskebi wajônemoodiza etc.	Perhaps they had etc.

This tense is also used for the *past indefinite* and *pluperfect* tenses.

Future.

Wskebiji wajônema.	Perhaps I will have.

etc., as in the *present* tense, placing *wskebiji* before the verb.

Second Future.

Wskebiji kizi wajônema.	Perhaps I will have had.

etc. after the *simple future,* putting *wskebiji kizi* before the verb.

Conditional Mood.

Present.

Wskebiba wajônema.	Perhaps I would have

etc., after the *present* tense, putting always *wskebiba* before the verb.

Past.

Wskebiba wajônemôza	Perhaps I would have had.

etc., after the *imperfect* tense, commencing by wskebiba.

SUBJUNCTIVE MOOD.

Present.

Wskebiba wajônemôna.	Perhaps if I have.
" wajônemana.	" if thou hast.
" wajônega.	" if he has.
" wajônemaga.	" if we have.
" wajônemgua	" if you have.
" wajônemoodida.	" if they have.

Imperfect.

Wskebiba wajônemôshôna.	Perhaps if I had.
Wskebiba wajônemashana.	" if thou hadst.
Wskebiba wajônegeshana.	" if he had.
Wskebiba wajônemageshana.	" if we had.
Wskebiba wajônemagueshana.	" if you had.
Wsbebiba wajônemoôdishana.	" if they had.

Pluperfect.

Wskebiba kizi wajône-môshôna.	Perhaps if I had had.

etc., after the *imperfect*, always placing *kizi* between *wskebiba* and the *verb.*

DUBITATIVE—NEGATIVE

Of the two foregoing dubitative Conjugations (*Literal*).

INDICATIVE MOOD.

Present.

Walma wajônok ases.	Perhaps I have no horse.
Walma wajônema môni.	Perhaps I have no money.

etc., after the *present* tense of the *dubitative*, always commencing by *walma* instead of *wskebi.*

Imperfect.

Walma wajônokza miguen.	Perhaps I had no pen.
Walma wajonemôza pilaskw.	Perhaps I had no paper.

etc., after the *imperfect* of the *dubitative*, here too commencing always by *walma*.

Future.

Walmaji wajônok tôbi.	Perhaps I will have no bow.
Walmaji wajônema pakua.	Perhaps I will have no arrow.

etc. as in the *Present* tense, changing *walma* into *walmaji*.

Conditional Mood.

Present.

Walmaba wajônôk wdahogan.	Perhaps I should have no paddle.
Walmaba wajônema wiguaol.	Perhaps I should have no canoe.

etc., after the *ind. present* of the *dubitative*.

CONJUGATION OF THE VERB,

Aimuk, to be. *

Indicative Mood.

Present.

N'-d-ai wigwômek.	I am in the house.
K-d-ai etc.	Thou art etc.
Ao etc.	He (she) is etc.
N'-d-aibena etc.	We are etc.
K'-d-aiba etc.	You are etc.
Aaok etc.	They are etc.

(*Negative*: ôda *n'-d-aiw*, ôda *aiwi*, I am not, he is not).

---

* Note.—This *verb* is not *an auxiliary*, but a *principal* verb, which denotes *presence* or *residence*.

Imperfect.

N'-d-aib aiamihawiga-migok.	I was in the church.
K'-d-aib etc.	Thou wast etc.
'Aob etc.	He was etc.
N'-d-aibenob etc.	We were etc.
K'-d-aibôb etc.	You were etc.
'Aobanik etc.	They were etc.

This tense is also used for the *past* definite.

Future.

N'-d-aiji Molian.	I shall or will be in Montreal.
K'-d-aiji etc.	Thou wilt be etc.
'Aoji etc.	He will be etc.
N'-d-aibenaji etc.	We shall be etc.
K'-d-aibaji etc.	You will be etc.
'Aoakji etc.	They will be etc.

Second Future.

N'-d-aiji kizi wigiak. . .	I shall be at home already.

etc., after the *simple future*, putting *kizi* after the verb.

CONDITIONAL MOOD.

Present.

N'daiba kpiwi.	I should be in the woods
K'-d-aiba etc.	Thou wouldst be etc.
'Aoba etc.	He would be etc.
N'-d-aibenaba etc.	We should be etc.
K'd-aibaba etc.	You would etc.
'Aoakba.	They would be etc.

Past.

N'-d-aibba odanak.	I should have been in town.
K'-d-aibba etc.	Thou wouldst have been etc.

'Aobba etc.	He would have been etc.
N'-d-aibenobba etc.	We should have been etc.
K'-d-aibôbba etc.	You would have been etc.
'Aobanikba etc.	They would have been etc.

IMPERATIVE MOOD.

Ai.	Be, stay *or* remain.
Aij.	Let him be *or* remain.
Aida.	Let us be *or* remain.
Aigw.	Be *or* remain.
Aidij.	Let them be *or* remain.

SUBJUNCTIVE MOOD.

Present.

(*Chowaldôzo*)	(*Some want*)
N'-d-ain.	That I may be *or* remain.
K'-d-ain.	That thou mayest be *or* remain.
W'-d-ain.	That he may be *or* remain.
N'-d-ainana.	That we may be *or* remain.
K'-d-ainô.	That you may be *or* remain.
W'-d-ainô.	That they may be *or* remain.

Imperfect.

(*Chowaldôzoba*)	(*Some wanted*)
N'-d-ainaza.	That I might be *or* remain.
W'-d-ainaza.	That he might be *or* remain.
N'-d-ainanossa.	That we might be *or* remain.
K'-d-ainôssa.	That you might be *or* remain.
W'-d-ainôssa.	That they might be *or* remain.

Past.

Kizi n'-d-ain.	That I may have been *or* remained.

etc., after the *present*, commencing by *kizi*.

Pluperfect.

Kizi n'-d-ainaza.	That I might have been *or* resided.

etc., after the *imperfect*, commencing always by *kizi.*

CONJUGATION OF THE *ANIMATE* OBJECTIVE VERB.

Namihômuk, to see.

(Indefinite Conjugation).

INDICATIVE MOOD.

Present.

N'namihô, mosbas.	I see a mink.
K'namihô etc.	Thou seest etc.
'Namiha *	He sees etc.
N'namihôbena etc.	We see etc.
K'namihôba etc.	You see etc.
'Namihak *	They see etc.

Imperfect.

N'namihôb moskuas.	I saw, a muskrat.
K'namihôb etc.	Thou sawest etc.
'Namihab *	He saw etc.
N'namihôbenob etc.	We saw etc.
K'namihôbôb etc.	You saw etc.
'Namihabanik *	The saw etc.

Past definite.

N'namihôôb mateguas.	I saw a hare.
K'namihôôb etc.	Thou sawest etc.
'Namihab *	He saw etc.
N'namihôbenoob etc.	We saw etc.

---

* Say: 'namiha, 'namihak, *mosbisa;* 'namihab, 'namihabanik, *moskuasa;—maleguasa.*

K'namihôbôôb etc.	You saw etc.
'Namihabanik *	They saw etc.

Past Indefinite.

N'kizi namihô awasos.	I have seen a bear.
'Kizi namiha. *	He has seen etc.
N'kizi namihôbena etc.	We have seen etc.
K'kizi namihôba etc.	You have seen etc.
'Kizi namihak. *	They have seen etc.

Pluperfect.

N'kizi namihôb peziko.	I had seen a buffalo.
K'kizi namihôb etc.	Thou hadst seen etc.
'Kizi namihab. *	He had seen etc.
N'kizi namihôbenob etc.	We had seen etc.
K'kizi namihôbôb etc.	You had seen etc.
'Kizi namihabanik. *	They had seen etc.

Future.

N'namihôji môlsem.	I shall or will see a wolf.
K'namihôji etc.	Thou wilt see etc.
'Namihaji. †	He will see etc.
N'namihôbenaji etc.	We shall see etc.
K'namihôbaji etc.	You will see etc.
'Namihakji. *	They will see etc.

Second Future.

N'namihôji kizi wnegigw.	I shall or will have seen an otter.
K'namihôji kizi etc.	Thou wilt have seen etc.
'Namihaji kizi. *	He will have seen etc.
N'namihôbenaji kizi etc.	We shall have seen etc.

---

* Say: 'namiha, 'namihak, *mosbisa;* 'namihab, 'namihabanik, *moskuasa;—maleguasa.*
† Say: namiha,—namihak *awasosa;*—namihab,—namiha-banik, *pesikoa;* 'namihaji, 'namihakji, *môlsemo;* 'namihaji,—'namihakji kizi, *wnegigwa.*

K'namihôbaji kizi etc.	You will h. seen etc.
'Namihakji kizi. *	They will h. seen etc.

Conditional Mood.

Present.

N'namihôba magôlibo.	I should see a carribou.
N'namihôba etc.	Thou wouldst see etc.
'Namihaba †	He would see etc.
N'namihôbenaba etc.	We should see etc.
K'namihôbaba etc.	You would see etc.
'Namihakba †	They would see etc.

Past.

N'namihôbba nolka.	I should have seen a deer.
K'namihôbba etc.	Thou wouldst have seen etc.
Namihabba etc.	He would have seen etc.
N'amihôbenobba etc.	We should have seen etc.
K'namihôbôbba etc.	You would have seen etc.
'Namihabanikba etc.	They would have seen etc.

Imperative Mood.

Namiha.	See (thou).
Namihôj.	Let him see.
Namihôda.	Let us see.
Namihokw.	See (ye or you).
Namihôdij.	Let them see.

Subjunctive Mood.

Present.

N'namihôn.	That I may see.
K'namihôn.	That thou mayest see.

---

* Say: namiha,—namihak *awasosa;*—namihab,—namiha-banik, *pesikoa;* 'namihaji, 'namihakji, *môlsemo;* 'namihaji,—'namihakji kizi, *wnegigwa.*

† Say: 'namihaba, 'namihakba, *magôliboa.*

W'namihôn.	That he may see.
N'namihônana.	That we may see.
K'namihônô.	That you may see.
W'namihônô.	That they may see.

Imperfect.

N'namihônaza.	That I might see.
K'namihônaza.	That thou mightest see.
W'namihônaza.	That he might see.
N'namihônanossa.	That we might see.
K'namihônôssa.	That you might see.
W'namihônôssa.	That they might see.

Past.

Kizi n'namihôn,	That I may have seen.

etc., as above, after the *present* commencing by *kizi*.

Pluperfect.

Kizi n'namihônaza,	That I might have seen

etc., after the *imperfect*, commencing by *kizi*.

CONJUGATION OF THE *ANIMATE* OBJECTIVE VERB,

Namihómuk, to see.

(*Finite Conjugation*).

INDICATIVE MOOD.

Present.

N'namihô alnôba.	I see the indian.
K'namihô etc.	Thou seest etc.
W'namihô etc.	He sees etc.
N'namihônna etc.	We see etc.

K'namihôwô etc.	You see etc.
W'namihôwô etc.	They see. etc.

Imperfect.

N'namihôb plachmôn.	I saw the frenchman.
K'namihôb etc.	Thou sawest etc.
W'namihôbani.*	He saw etc.
N'namihônnob etc.	We saw etc.
K'namihôwôb etc.	You saw etc.
W'namihôwôbani*	They saw etc.

Past definite.

N'namihôôb pastoni.	I saw the american.
K'namihôôb etc.	Thou sawest etc.
W'namihôbani *	He saw etc.
N'namihônôôb etc.	We saw etc.
K'namihôwôb etc.	You saw etc.
W'namihôwôbani *	They saw etc.

Past Indefinite.

N'kizi namihô iglismôn.	I have seen the englishman.
K'kzi namihô etc.	Thou hast seen etc.
W'kizi namihô †	He has seen etc.
N'kizi mamihônna etc.	We have seen etc.
K'kizi namihôwô etc.	You have seen etc.
W'kizi namihôwô †	They have seen etc.

Pluperfect.

N'kizi memihôb alemôn.	I had seen the german.
K'kizi namihôb etc.	Thou hadst seen etc.
W'kizi mamihôbani ‡ etc.	He had seen the etc.

---

* Say: w'namihôbaui, w'namihôwôbani *plachmôna;—pastonia.*

† Say: w'kizi namihô,—namihôwô *iglismôna.*

‡ Say: w'kizi namihôbani, namihôwôbani, *alemóna;* w'namihôji, w'namihowôji, kaptina.

N'kizi namihônnob etc.	We had seen etc.
K'kizi namihowôb etc.	You had seen etc.
W'kizi namihôwôbani *	They had seen etc.

Future.

N'namiliôji kaptin.	I shall or will see the captain.
K'namchôji etc.	Thou wilt see etc.
W'namhôji * etc.	He will see etc.
N'namihômaji etc.	We shall see etc.
K'namihôwôji etc.	You will see etc.
W'namihôwôji *	They will see etc.

Second Future.

N'namihôji kizi nojinbizonhowad.	I shall or will have seen the doctor.
K'namihôji kizi etc.	Thou wilt have seen etc.
W'namihôji kizi †	He will have seen etc.
N'namihômaji kizi etc.	We shall have seen etc.
K'namihôwôji kizi etc.	You will have seen etc.
W'namihôwôji kizi nojinbizonhowaliji.	They will have seen etc.

CONDITIONAL MOOD.

Present.

N'namihôba soghe-bad.	I should see the inn-keeper.
W'namihôba.‡	He would see etc.
N'namihônnaba etc.	We should see etc.
K'namihôwôba etc.	You would see etc.
W'namihôwôba.‡	They would see etc.

---

* Say: w'kizi namihôbani, namihôwôbani, *alemóna;* w'namihôji, w'namihowôji, kaptina.

† W'namihôji kizi *noji–nbizonhowaliji.*

‡ W'namihôba, w'namihôwôba, *soghebaliji;*

Past.

N'namihôbba notkuaag.	I should have seen the pilot.
W'namihôbaniba.*	He would have seen etc.
N'namihônnobba etc.	We should have seen etc.
K'namihôwôbba etc.	You would have seen etc.
W'namihôwôbaniba *	They would have seen etc.

The remaining *Moods* and *tenses* are to be conjugated as in the *indefinite* conjugation.

CONJUGATION.

Of the *inanimate* objective verb, *namitozik*, to see
(*Indefinite Conjugation*).

INDICATIVE MOOD.

Present.

N'namito wigwôm.	I see a house.
'Namito etc.	He sees etc.
N'namitobena etc.	We see etc.
K'namitoba etc.	You see etc.
'Namitoak etc.	They see etc.

Imperfect.

N'namitob mdawagen	I saw a flag.
'Namitob etc.	He saw etc.
N'namitobenob etc.	We saw etc.
K'namitobôb etc.	You saw etc.
'Namitobanik etc.	They saw etc.

Past definite.

N'namitoob odana.	I saw a city, village.
'Namitob etc.	He saw etc.

---

* W'namihôbaniba, w'namihôwobaniba *nolkuaagi.*

N'namitobenoob etc.	We saw etc.
K'namitobôôb etc.	You saw etc.
'Namitobanik etc.	They saw etc.

Past—.Indefinite.

N'kizi namito awighigan.	I have seen a book, a deed.
'Kizi namito etc.	He has seen etc.
N'kizi namitobena etc.	We have seen etc.
K'kizi namitoba etc.	You have seen etc.
'Kizi namitoak etc.	They have seen etc.

Pluperfect.

N'kizi namitob ktolagw	I had seen a ship.
'Kizi namitob.	He had seen etc.
N'kizi namitobenob.	We had seen etc.
K'kizi namitobôb.	You had seen etc.
'Kizi namitobanik.	They had seen etc.

Future.

N'namitoji kebahodwigamigw.	I shall or will see a jail.
'Namitoji.	He will see etc.
N'namitobenaji.	We shall see etc.
K'namitobaji.	You will see etc.
'Namitoakji.	They will see etc.

Second Future.

N'namitoji kizi aiami- hawigamigw.	I shall have seen a church.
'Namitoji kizi.	He will have seen etc.
N'namitobenaji kizi.	We shall have seen etc.
K'namitobaji kizi.	You will have seen etc.
'Namitoakji kizi.	They will have seen etc.

Conditional Mood.

Present.

N'namitoba, sibo.	I should see a river.
'Namitoba.	He would see etc.
N'namitobenaba.	We should see etc.
K'namitobaba.	You would see etc.
'Namitoakba.	They would see etc.

Past.

N'namitobba nebes.	I should have seen a lake.
'Namitobba.	He would have s. etc.
N'namitobenobba.	We should have seen etc.
K'namitobôbba.	You would have seen etc.
'Namitobanikba.	They would have seen etc.

Imperative Mood.

Namito.	See (thou).
Namitoj.	Let him see.
Namitoda.	Let us see.
Namitogw.	See (ye or you).
Namitodij.	Let them see.

Subjunctive Mood.

Present.

N'namiton.	That may see.
W'namiton.	That he may see.
N'namitonana.	That we may see.
K'namitonô.	That you may see.
W'namitonô.	That they may see.

Imperfect.

N'namitonaza.	That I might see.
W'namitonaza.	That he might see.

N'namitonanossa.	That we might see.
K'namitonôssa.	That you might see.
W'namitonôssa.	That they might see.

Past.

Kizi n'namiton.	That I may have seen.

etc., after the *present*, commencing by *kizi*.

Pluperfect.

Kizi n'namitonaza.	That I might have seen.

etc., after the *imperfect*, commencing by *kizi*.

CONJUGATION OF THE *INANIMATE* OBJECTIVE VERB,

Namitôzik, to see.

(*Finite Conjugation*).

INDICATIVE MOOD.

Present.

N'namiton paskhigan.	I see the gun.
N'namitonana etc.	We see etc.
K'namitonô etc.	You see etc.
W'namitonô etc.	They see etc.

Imperfect.

N'namitonab saguôlhigan.	I saw the ramrod.
N'namitonanob etc. ⎫	We saw etc.
K'namitonanob etc. ⎭	
K'namitonôb etc.	You saw etc.
W'namitonôb etc.	They saw etc.

This tense is also used for the *past definite*.

N'kizi namiton adebôlagw.	I have seen the rifle.
N'kizi namitonana etc.	We have seen etc.
K'kizi namitonô etc.	You have seen etc.
W'kizi namitonô etc.	They have seen etc.

Pluperfect.

N'kizi namitonab chawapnigan.	I had seen the fish hook
N'kizi namitonanob etc.	We had seen etc.
K'kizi namitonôb etc.	You had seen etc.
W'kizi namitonôb etc.	They had seen etc.

Future.

N'namitonji chawaniganakuam.	I shall see the fishing rod.
N'namitonanaji etc.	We shall see etc.
K'namitonôji etc.	You will see etc.
W'namitonôji etc.	They will see etc.

Second Future.

N'namitonji kizi chawapniganatagw.	I shall have seen the fishing line.
N'namitonanaji kizi etc.	We shall have seen etc.
K'namitonôji kizi etc.	You will have seen etc.
W'namitonôji kizi etc.	They will h. seen etc.

CONDITIONAL MOOD.

Present.

N'namitonba aiamihawigamigw.	I should see the church.
N'namitonanaba etc.	We should see etc.
K'namitonôba etc.	You would see etc.
W'namitonôba etc.	They would see etc.

N'namitonabba sahôkuahigan.	I should have seen the bell.
N'namitonanobba etc.	We should have seen etc.
K'namitonôbba etc.	You would have seen etc.
W'namitonôbba etc.	They would have seen etc.

The remaining *moods* and *tenses* are to be conjugated as in the *indefinite* conjugation.

CONJUGATION OF THE PASSIVE VERB,

Kazalmegwzimuk, to be loved.

INDICATIVE MOOD.

Present.

N'kezalmegwzi.	I am loved.
'Kezalmegwzo.	He is loved.
N'kezalmegwzibena.	We are loved.
K'kezalmegwziba.	You are loved.
'Kezalmegwzoak	They are loved.

Imperfect.

N'kezalmegwzib.	I was loved.
'Kezalmegwzob.	He was loved.
N'kezalmegwzibenob.	We were loved.
K'kezalmegwzibôb.	You were loved.
'Kezalmegwzobanik.	They were loved.

This tense is also used for the *past definite*, *indefinite* and *pluperfect* tenses.

Future.

N'kezalmegwziji.	I shall *or* will be loved.

etc., after the *present* tense, affixing *ji* to the verb.

Conditional Mood.

Present.

N'kezalmegwziba | I should be loved.
  etc., after the *present* tense, affixing *ba* to the verb.

Past.

N'kezalmegwzibba. | I should have been loved
  etc., after the *imperfect* tense, affixing *ba* to the verb.

Imperative Mood.

Kezalmegwzi.	Be (thou) loved.
Kezalmegwzij.	Let him be loved.
Kezalmegwzida.	Let us be loved.
Kezalmegwzigw.	Be (ye *or* you) loved.
Kezalmegwzidij.	Let them be loved.

Subjunctive Mood.

Present.

N'kezalmegwzin.	That I may be loved.
W'kezalmegwzin.	That he may etc.
N'kezalmegwzinana.	That we may etc.
K'kezalmegwzinô.	That you may etc.
W'kezalmegwzinô.	That they may etc.

Imperfect.

N'kezalmegwzinaza.	That I might be loved.
W'kezalmegwzinaza.	That he might etc.
N'kazalmegwzinanossa	That we might etc.
K'kezalmegwzinôssa.	That you might etc.
W'kezalmegwzinôssa.	That they might etc.

This tense is used also for the two remaining tenses.

RELATIVE CONJUGATION

Of the verb *Kazalmômuk*, to love, affirmative form.

(I. . . thee, etc.)

INDICATIVE MOOD.

Present.

K'kezalmel.	I love thee.
K'kezalmelbena.	We love thee.
K'kezalmegw.	He loves thee.
K'kezalmegok.	They love thee.
K'kezalmelba.	I love you.
K'kezalmebena.	We love you.
K'kezalmegwô.	He loves you.
K'kezalmegwôk.	They love you.

Imperfect.

K'kezalmelob.	I loved thee.
K'kezalmelbenop.	We loved thee.
K'kezalmegob.	He loved thee.
K'kezalmegobanik.	They loved thee.
K'kezalmelbôp.	I loved you.
K'kezalmelbenop.	We loved you.
K'kezalmegwôp.	He loved you.
K'kezalmegwôbanik.	They loved you.

This tense is used also for past *definite*, past *indefinite* and *pluperfect* tenses.

(Negative.—Present)

O'da k'kezalmelo.	I don't love thee.
" k'kezalmeloppena.	We don't love thee.
" k'kezalmegowi.	He does not love thee
" k'kezalmegowiak.	They don't love thee.
" k'kezalmeloppa.	I don't love you.

"   k'kezalmeloppena. | We don't love you.
O'da k'kezalmegowiwwô. | He does not love you.
O'da k'kezalmegowiwwôk. | They don't love you.

(*Imperfect*).

O'da k'kezalmelob.   I did not love you.

   etc., after the affirmative form, *imperfect* tense, commencing always by *ôda*.

RELATIVE CONJUGATION

Of the verb *Kazalmômule*, to love, affirmative form.

(*Thou. . . me, etc.*)

Indicative Mood.

Present.

K'kezalmi. | Thou lovest me.
K'kezalmiba. | You love me.
N'kezalmegw. | He loves me.
N'kezalmegok. | They love me.
K'kezalmibena. | Thou lovest us.
K'kezalmibena. | You love us.
N'kezalmegonna. | He loves us.
N'kezalmegonnawak. | They love us.

Imperfect.

K'kezalmib. | Thou lovedst me.
K'kezalmibôp. | You loved me.
N'kezalmegob. | He loved me.
N'kezalmegobanik. | They loved me.
K'kezalmibenop. | Thou lovedest us.
K'kezalmibenop. | You loved us.
N'kezalmegonnop. | He loved us.
N'kezalmegonnobanik. | They loved us.

This tense is used also for past *definite*, past *indefinite* and *pluperfect* tenses.

(*Negative.—Present*).

O'da k'kezalmiw.		Thou doest not love me.
"	k'kezalmippa.	You don't love me.
"	n'kezalmegowi.	He does not love me.
"	n'kezalmegowiak.	They don't love me.
"	k'kezalmippena.	Thou doest not love us.
"	k'kezalmippena.	You don't love us.
"	n'kezalmegowinna.	He does not love us.
"	n'kezalmegowinnawak.	They don't love us.

Imperfect.

O'da k'kezalmib. | Thou didst not love me.

etc., after the affirmative form, *imperfect* tense commencing always by *ôda.*

LIST OF SOME OF THE VERBS MOST FREQUENTLY MET WITH IN THE ABENAKIS LANGUAGE.

Infinitive.	Signification.	Imp. 2 pers. sing.	Imp. 2 pers. plur.
Agimômuk,	To count;	Agima,	Agimogw.
Agidôzik,*	To read.*	Agida,	Agidamogw.
Agizimuk,*		Agizi,	Agizigw.
Awighômuk,	To mark;	Awigha,	Awighogw.
Awighôzilk,*	To write.*	do	Awighamogw.
Awighigamuk,*		Awighiga,	Awighigagw.
Agakimômuk,	To teach.	Agakima,	Agakimogw.
Agakigamimuk,		Agakigami.	Agakigamigw.
Alokamuk,	To work.	Aloka,	Alokagw.
Awakamuk,	To use;	Awaka,	Awakagw.
Awakatôzik,	To employ.	Awakato,	Awakatogw.
Askawihômuk,	To wait for;	Skawiha,	Skawihogw.
Askawitôzik,	To expect.	Skawito,	Skawitogw.
Awigihômuk,	To appease.	Awigitha,	Awigihogw.
Akikamuk,	To sow.	Kika,	Kikagw.
Aliguawômuk,		Liguawa,	Liguaogw.
Aliguôzik,	To sew.	Ligua,	Liguamogw.
Aliguônsamuk,		Liguônsa,	Liguônsagw.

Awskônômuk, }	To displace.	Awskôna,	Awskônogw.
Awskônôzik,		do	Awskônemogw.
Awskônkamuk,	To trouble.	Awskônka,	Awskônkagw.
Alidahômômuk,	To think;	Lidahôma,	Lidahômogw.
Alidahôdôzik,	To presume.	Lidahôda,	Lidahôdamogw.
Alidahôzimuk,		Lidahôzi,	Lidahôzigw.
Channômuk,* }	To stop; a arrest.*	Channa,	Channogw.
Channozik,*		do	Channemogw.
Chanosamuk, }		Chanosa,	Chanosagw.
Chegasômuk, }	To light.	Chegasa,	Chegasogw.
Chegasôzik,	To burn.	do	Chegasmogw.
Idôzik,	To say.	Ida,	Idamogw.
Ikôlômuk, }	To defend.	Ikôla,	Ikôlogw.
Ikôdôzik,		Ikôda,	Ikôdemogw.
Ikôlwamuk, }	To defend oneself.	Ikôlwa,	Ikôlwagw.
Ikôlzimuk,	To defend each other.	Ikôlzi,	Ikôlzigw.
Ikôldimuk,			Ikôldigw.
Kalolômuk,	To speak to.	Kelola,	Kelologw.
Kalozimuk,	To talk, speak.	Kelozi,	Kelozigw.
Kawimuk,	To sleep.	Kawi,	Kawigw.
Kwilawahômuk, }	To look for.	Kwilawaha,	Kwilawahogw.
Kwilawatôzik,	To search.	Kwilawato,	Kwilawatogw.

LIST OF VERBS.—(*Continued*).

Infinitive.	*Signification.*	*Imp. 2 pers. sing.*	*Imp. 2 pers. plur.*
Kawhômuk,	To cut down (a tree).	Kawha,	Kawhogw.
Kawhakuamuk,	A tree.	Kawhakua,	Kawhakuagw.
Kajimijebikamuk,	To unload.	Kajimijebika,	Kajimijebikagw.
Kebikwahômuk,	To seal.	Kebikwaha,	Kebikwahogw.
Kebikwahôzik,		do	Kebikwaamogw.
Kebikwahigamuk,		Kebikwahiga,	Kebikwahigagw.
Kabhômuk,*	To shut; to cork.	Kebaha,	Kebahogw.
Kabhôzik,	To emprison.*	do	Kebahamogw.
Kazebaalômuk,	To wash.	Kezebaala,	Kezebaalogw.
Kazebaadôzik,		Kezebaado,	Kezebaadogw.
Kazebaadigamuk,		Kezebaadiga,	Kezebaadigagw.
Kwalbenômuk,	To turn (over).	Kwelbena,	Kwelbenogw.
Kwalbenôzik,		do	Kwelbenemogw.
Kwalbosamuk,	To turn round.	Kwelbosa,	Kwelbosagw.
Kwazialômuk,	To swallow.	Kweziala,	Kwezialogw.
Kwaziadôzik,		Kweziado,	Kweziadogw.
Kwaziadômuk,		Kweziado,	Kweziadôgw.
Kadopimuk,	To be hungry.	Kadopi,	Kadopigw.
Kadawesmimuk,	To be thirsty, dry.	Kadawesmi.	Kadawesmigw.

Kitalômuk,	To whet;	Kitala,	Kitalogw.
Kitadôzik,	To sharpen.	Kitado,	Kitadogw.
Kitadasimuk,		Kitadasi,	Kitadasigw.
Kadkahômuk,	To dig;	Kadkaha,	Kadkahogw.
Kadkahôzik,	To dig out.	do	Kadkahamogw.
Kadkahigamuk,		Kadkahiga,	Kadkahigragw.
Kalabilômuk,	To tie (up).	Kelabila,	Kelabilogw.
Kalabidôzik,		Kelabido,	Kelabidogw.
Kalabligamuk,		Kelabliga,	Kelabligagw.
Kaboakwhômuk,	To button (up).	Keboakwha,	Keboakwhogw.
Kaboakwhôzik,		do	Keboakwhamogw.
Kwaguenômuk,	To push.	Kwaguena,	Kwaguenogw.
Kwagwnôzik,		do	Kwagwnemogw.
Kadosmimuk,	To drink.	Kadosmi,	Kadosmigw.
Kwaguatskoalômuk,	To try.	Kwaguatskoala,	Kwaguatskoalogw.
Kwaguatskoadôzik,		Kwaguatskoado,	Kwaguatskoadodgw.
Kwôzolômuk,	To shun;	Kwôzola,	Kwôzologw.
Kwôzodôzik,	To avoid.	Kwôzoda,	Kwôzodamogw.
Kazalmômuk,	To love; to like.	Kezalma,	Kezalmogw.
Kazaldôzik,		Kezalda,	Kezaldamogw.
Kazalgamuk,		Kezalga,	Kezalgagw.
Kalajimuk,	To freeze.	Kelaji,	Kelajigw.

LIST OF VERBS.—(Continued).

Infinitive.	Signification.	Imp. 2 pers. sing.	Imp. 2 pers. plur.
Kôttassimuk, } Kôttôzik, } Kôttômuk, }	To hide; To conceal.	Kôttasi, Kôtto, Kôtla,	Kôtasigw. Kôttogw. Kôtlogw.
Kagalnômuk, } Kagalnôzik, }	To hold.	Kagalna, do	Kagalnogw. Kagalnemogw.
Kazômahlômuk,	To run.	Kezômahlô,	Kezômahlôgw.
Kamodnamuk,	To steal.	Kemodna,	Kemodnagw.
Kôgôlwamuk,	To cry, to halloo.	Kôgôlwa,	Kôgôlwagw.
Kawhoamuk,	To win.	Kawhoa,	Kawhoagw.
Mohômuk, } Mijôzik, } Mitsimuk, }	To eat.	Moha, Miji, Mitsi,	Mohogw. Mijigw. Mitsigw.
Magamuk,	To give (away).	Maga,	Magagw.
Môjahômuk, } Môjatôzik, }	To begin.	Môjaha, Môjato,	Môjahogw. Môjatogw.
Môjalômuk, } Môjadôzik, }	To carry away, To take away.	Môjala, Môja lo,	Môjalogw. Môjadogw.
Mahsihômuk, } Mahsitôzik, }	To make greater.	Msiha, Msito,	Msihogw. Msitogw.

Madwôzimuk,	{ To complain; { To grumble.	Madwôzi,	Madwôzigw.
Manohômuk, Manohôzik, }	To buy.	Manoha, do	Manahogw. Manohomogw.
Manohigamuk,		Manohiga,	Manohigagw.
Migakamuk,	To fight.	Migaka,	Migakagw.
Malisjômuk,	To weep.	Melisjô,	Melisjôgw.
Manazaawimuk,	To be saving; to save.	Manazaawi,	Manazaawigw.
Mijebikamuk,	To load.	Mijebika,	Mijebikagw.
Mômjimômuk,	To congratulate.	Mimjima,	Mômimogw.
Mômjidimuk,	{ To congratulate one { another.		Mômjidigw.
Maskawlohômuk, Maskawlohôzik, }	To praise.	Mskawloha, do	Mskawlohogw. Mskawlohmogw.
Môjimuk,	To start, to go away.	Môji,	Môjigw.
Naslômuk, }	To put on.	Nasla,	Naslogw.
Nastôzik, }		Nasto,	Nastogw.
Nimskawômuk, } Nimskôzik, }	To fetch.	Nimskawa, Nimska;	Nimskawogw. Nimskamogw.
Naskuahômuk,	To comb.	Naskuaha,	Naskuahogw.
Naskuahozimuk,	To comb oneself.	Naskuahozi,	Naskuahozigw.
Nadomômuk, } Nadodôzik, }	To inquire, to ask for.	Nadoma, Nadoda,	Nadomogw. Nadodemogw.

LIST OF VERBS.—(*Continued*).

Infinitive.	Signification.	Imp. 2 pers. sing.	Imp. 2 pers. plur.
Nadodemawômuk,	To ask; to question.	Nadodemawa,	Nadodemawogw.
Nadodemokamuk,	To ask for, to inquire.	Nadodemoka,	Nadodemokagw.
Nosokawômuk,		Nosokawa,	Nosokawogw.
Nosokôzik, †	To follow, to run after.	Nosoka,	Nosokamogw.
Nosokozimuk,		Nosokozi,	Nosokozigw.
Nanawalmômuk,		Nanawalma,	Nanawalmogw.
Nanawaldôzik,	To keep; to take care of	Nanawalda,	Nanawaldamogw.
Namihômuk,		Namiha,	Namihogw.
Namitôzik,	To see; to observe.	Namito,	Namitogw.
Pazôbimuk,		Pazôbi,	Pazôbigw.
Namitlowamuk.	To show.	Namitlowa,	Namitlowagw.
Nadialimuk,	To hunt.	Nadiali,	Nadialigw.
Nakasahôzik,	To put out.	Nkasaha,	Nkasahamogw.
Ojemimuk.	To relate; to declare.	O'jemi,	O'jemigw.
O'tlômuk,	To more forward.	O'tla,	O'tlogw.
O'ttôzik,	To adjourn.	O'tto,	O'ttogw.

† NOTE.—As you see, many of these *infinitives* are expressed in *two* and *three* different ways, having however the same signification in English; these verbs are: 1. the *animate*, ending in *muk*; 2 the *inanimate*, ending in *zik*; 3. the *neuter*, ending in *zik*; the *neuter*, ending, like the animate, in *muk*. See Conjugations.

O'benômuk, } O'benôzik, }	To untie.	O'bena, do	O'benogw. O'bnemogw.
O'dokôlômuk,	To declare one's fault.	O'dokôla,	O'dokôlogw.
O'dokôdôzik,	To explain.	O'dokôda,	O'dokôdamogw.
O'bankamuk,	To pay.	O'banka,	O'bankagw.
O'nkohlômuk,	To sell.	O'nkohlô.	O'nkohlôgw.
O'mawômuk, } O'mamuk, }	To converse.	O'mawa, O'ma,	O'maogw. O'magw.
O'dokazimuk,	To come; to arrive.	O'dokazi,	O'dokazigw
Paiômuk,		Paiô,	Paiôgw.
Ponômuk, } Ponôzik, }	To put; to place.	Pona, do	Ponogw. Ponemogw.
Ponasimuk, }		Ponasi,	Ponasigw.
Pitkazawamuk,	{ To load a gun, a canon, a pistol.	Pitkazawa,	Pitkazawagw.
Pakôgnômuk, } Pakôgnôzik, }	To bend.	Pkôgna, do	Pkôgnogw. Pkôgnemogw.
Pakawagnômuk, } Pakawagnôzik, }	To fold; to plait.	Pkawagna. do	Pkawagnogw. Pkawagnemogw.
Pasktahôzik,	To shell; to break.	Pasktaha,	Pasktahamogw.
Poskenômuk,	To bury.	Poskena,	Poskenogw.
Poskwenômuk, } Poskwenôzik, }	To break; to revoke.	Poskwena, do	Poskwenog. Poskwenemogw

LIST OF VERBS.—(Continued).

Infinitive.	Signification.	Imp. 2 pers. sing.	Imp. 2 pers. plur.
Pazwômuk, } Padôzik, }	To bring.	Pazowa.	Pazoogw.
	To beat.	Pado,	Padogw.
Pôktahômuk,	To beat.	Pôktaha,	Pôktahogw.
Poskwtahômuk, } Poskwtahôzik, }	To cut, (with an axe).	Poskwtaha, do	Poskwtahogw, Poskwtahamogw.
Poskwezômuk, } Poskwezôzik, }	To cut, (with a knife).	Poskweza, do	Poskwezogw. Poskwezemogw.
Poskwenômuk, } Poskwenôzik, }	To break, (with the hands).	Poskwena, do	Poskwenogw. Poskwenemogw.
Poskwkawômuk, }	To break, (with the feet).	Poskwkawa,	Poskwkaogw.
Poskwkôzik,* }	To infringe,* to transgress.	Poskwka,	Posbwkamogw.
Pakihômuk, } Pakitôzik. }	To clean; the clear.	Pakiha, Pakito,	Pakihogw. Pakitogw.
Palagzômuk, } Palagzôzik, }	To peel, (with knife).	Pelagza, do	Plagzogw. Plagzemogw.
Palagnômuk, } Palagnozik, }	To peel, (with the hands)	Plagna, do	Plagnogw. Plagnemogw.

Pakwsasômuk, }	To dry.	Pakwsasa,	Pakwsasogw.
Pakwsasôzik, }	To dry oneself.	do	Pakwsasmogw.
Pakwsasozimuk,		Pakwsasozi,	Pakwsasozigw.
Tamezômuk, }	To cut.	Tameza,	Temezogw.
Tamezôzik, }		do	Temezemogw.
Taakwenômuk, }	To shorten.	Taakwena,	Taakwenogw.
Taakwenôzik, }		do	Taakwenemogw.
Tapsedawômuk,	To listen to; to hear.	Tebestawa,	Tebestawogw.
Tapsedôzik,		Tebesta,	Tebestamogw.
Tapsedamasimuk,		Tebestamasi,	Tebestamasigw.
Tagamômuk, }	To strike.	Tagama,	Tagamogw.
Tagadôzik, }		Tagada,	Tagadamogw.
Tagamwamuk, }		Tagamwa.	Tagamwagw.
Wijokamômuk, }	To help; to assist.	Wijokama,	Wijokamogw.
Wijokadôzik, }	To help oneself.	Wijokada,	Wijokadamogw.
Wijokagamimuk,		Wijokagami,	Wijokagamigw.
Wijokamzimuk,		Wijokamzi,	Wijokamzigw.
Wijokadimuk,	To help other each.		Wijokadigw.
Wanialômuk, }	To lose.	Waniala,	Wanialogw.
Waniadôzik, }		Waniado,	Waniadogw.
Waniadômuk, }		Waniadô,	Waniadôgw.
Wikwnômuk, }	To draw, to take.	Wikwena,	Wikwenogw.
Wikwnôzik. }		do	Wikwenemogw.

LIST OF VERBS.—(*Continued*).

Infinitive.	Signification.	Imp. 2 pers. sing.	Imp. 2 pers. plur:
Wikomômuk, Wikodôzik, }	To ask for.	Wikoma. Wikoda,	Wikomogw. Wikodemogw.
Wawôdokawômuk, }	To warn; to notify.	Wawôdakawa,	Wawôdokawogw.
Wawôjemimuk,	To kiss.	Wawôjemi,	Wawôjemigw.
Wajamômuk, } Wajadôzik, }		Wajama, Wajada,	Wajamogw. Wajadamogw.
Walômasokamuk.	To swear (oath).	Wlômasoka.	Wlômasokagw.
Pasanlhômuk, } Pasantôzik.	To fill (up) with things.	Psanlha, Psanto,	Psanlhogw. Psantogw.
Pasanbaalômuk, } Pasanbaadôzik, }	To fill with liquid.	Psanbaala. Psanbaado,	Psanbaalogw. Psanbaadogw.
Pasanômkahômuk, } Pasanômkahôsik. }	To fill with sand or fine gravel.	Psanômkaha. do	Psanômkahogw. Psanômkamogw.
Pejidakamuk,	To forward; to mail.	Pejidaka.	Pejidakagw.
Siwanaômuk.	To salt.	Siwanaa, do	Siwanaogw. Siwanaamogw.
Siwanaôzik, Siwanaigamuk,		Siwanaiga,	Siwanaigagw.
Sinawwôdôzik, } Sinawwimuk, }	To sign.	Sinawwôda, Sinawwi,	Sinawwôdamogw. Sinawwigw.

Sagamômuk, Sagadôzik, Sagamwamuk,	To bite.	Sagama, Sagada, Sagamwa,	Sagamogw. Sagadamogw. Sagamwagw.
Sezohômuk, Sezohôzik, Sezohigamuk,	To paint.	Sezoha, do Sezohiga,	Sezohogw. Sezohomogw. Sezohigagw.
Taguaguiômuk Taguaguitôzik, Taguagualokamuk,	To finish; to terminate.	Taguaguia, Taguaguito, Taguagualoka,	Taguaguiogw. Taguagutiogw. Taguagualokagw.
Tablomômuk, Tablodôzik,	To mention.	Tebloma, Tebloda,	Teblomogw. Tablodmogw.
Talaginaalômuk, Talaginaadôzik,	To tear up.	Talaginaala, Talaginaado,	Talaginaalogw. Talaginaadogw.
Tablogamimuk,	To slander.	Teblogami,	Teblogamigw.
Wagiômuk, Wagitôzik,	To spoil; to endamage; to break.	Wagia, Wagito,	Wagiogw. Wagitogw.
Wagawnômuk, Wagawnôzik, Wagawnakamuk,	To disturb; to trouble.	Wagawna, do Wagawnaka,	Wagawnogw. Wagawnemogw. Wagawnakagw.
Wawimômuk,	To advise; to exhort.	Wawima,	Wawimogw.
Waliômuk, Walitôzik,	To make.	Wlia, Wlito,	Wliogw. Whitogw.

LIST OF VERBS.—(Continued).

Infinitive.	Signification.	Imp. 2 pers. sing.	Imp. 2 pers. plur.
Wanalmômuk, } Wanaldôzik,	To forget.	Wanalma, Wanalda,	Wanalmogw. Wanaldamogw.
Walilawaômuk, } Walilawatôzik,	To please, to content.	Wlilawaa, Wlilawato.	Wlilawaogw. Wlilawatogw.
Wadnômuk, } Wadnôzik,	To take.	Wdena, do	Wdenogw. Wdenemogw.
Walitebahlômuk, } Walitebahtôzik,	To set in order, to fix.	Wlitebahla, Wlitebahto,	Wlitebahlogw. Wlitebahtogw.
Wajônômuk, †} Wajônôzik,	To have.	Wajôna, do	Wajônogw. Wajônemogw.
Aimuk,*	To be.	Ai,	Aigw.

---

† Remember that *wajônômuk*, (to have) is not an auxiliary, but a principal verb expressing *possession.*

* *Aimuk* is likewise a principal verb, which denotes either *presence or residence.*

SYNOPTICAL ILLUSTRATIONS

SHOWING THE NUMEROUS MODIFICATIONS OF THE ABENAKIS VERB.

1. Transitive verb.—*Namihômuk*, to see, animate, *indefinite* conjugation:

N'namihô, n'namihô-bena tmakwa.	I see, we see a beaver.
'Namiha, namihak tmakwa.	He sees, they see a beaver, or beavers.

2. Transitive verb.—*Namihômuk*, to see, animate, *finite* conjugation:

N'namihô, n'namihônna tmakwa;	I see, we see the beaver;
W'namihô, w'namihôwô tmakwa.	He sees, they see the beaver, or beavers.

3. Transitive verb.—*Namilôzik*, to see, inanimate, *indefinite* conjugation:

N'namito, n'namitobena wiguaol;	I see, we see a bark canoe;
'Namito, 'namitoak wiguaol.	He sees, they see a bark canoe.

4. Transitive verb.—*Namitôzik*, to see, inanimate, *finite* conjugation:

N'namiton, n'namito-nana wiguaol;	I see, we see the bark canoe;
W'namiton, w'namitonô wiguaol.	He sees, they see the bark canoe.

5. Transitive verb.—*Pazôbimuk*, to see, *indefinite* conjugation:

N'pazôbi, n'pazôbibena nopahiwi;	I see, we see far off;
'Pazôbo, 'pazôboak nopahiwi.	He sees, they see far off.

6. Intransitive verb.—*Pazôbimuk*, to see, *finite* conjugation:

N'pazôbin, n'pazôbinana ia nebessek;	I see, we see clear down to that lake.

| W'pazôbin, w'pazôbinô ia nebessek. | He sees, they see clear down to that lake. |

7. Passive verb.—*Namiiguezimuk*, to be seen:

| N'namiiguezi, n'namiiguezibena; 'Namiiguezo, 'namiiguezoak. | I am seen, we are seen. He is seen, they are seen. |

8. Reflective verb—*Namihozimuk*, to see one self.

| N'namihozi n'namiho-*zibena*; 'Namihozo, 'namiho-zoak. | I see myself, we see ourselves; He sees himself, she sees herself, they see themselves. |

9. Communicative verb.—*Namihodimuk*, to see each other:

| N'namiho*dibena*, 'Namihodoak. | We see each other, They see each other, |

10. Causing verb.[*]—*Pazôbikhômuk*, va. to make see, (to restore a neighbour's sight), *definite* conjugation:

| N'pazôbikhô, n'pazôbikhônna manôdguezit; W'pazôbikhô, w'pazôbikhôwô nanôdgueziliji. | I make, we make the blind see, (we restore the blind man's sight); He makes, they make the blindman or blindmen see. |

11. Frequentative verb.—*Tôtagamômuk,* va. to strike repeatedly, (modification of the verb, *tagamômuk*, to strike,) animate, *finite* conjugation:

| N'tôtagamô, n'tôtagamônna; n'tôtagamôn-nawak; W'tôtagamô, w'tôtagamôwô. | I strike him, we strike him, repeatedly; we strike, them repeatedly; He strikes him, they strike them, repeatedly. |

---

[*] The causing verb indicates that its subject causes some animate object to *be* in a certain circumstance, or to do something, v. g. *n'kamgui*, I dive; *n'kamguikhô*, I make him dive.

12. Frequentative verb.—*Tôdagadôzik*, va, to strike repeatedly, (*modification* of the verb, *tagadôzik*, to strike,) inanimate, *finite* conjugation;

N'tôtagadamen, n'tôtagadamenana;	I strike it, we strike it, repeatedly.
W'tôtagadamen, w'totagadamenô.	He strikes it, they strike it, repeatedly.

13. Working verb.*—*Abaznodakamuk*, vn., to make baskets, derived from the substantive *abaznoda*, basket.

N'-d-abaznodaka, n'-d-abaznodakabena;	I make baskets, we make baskets;
'Abaznodaka, 'abazno dakak.	He makes baskets, they make baskets.

14. Slow-performing verb.—*Mannalokamuk*, vn., to work slowly, (1. *modification* of the verb *alokamuk*, to work):

N'mannaloka, n'manna-lokabena;	I work, we work, slowly;
N'mannawighiga, 'mannawighigak.	I write, they write, slowly.

15. Quick-performing verb.—*Kazalokamuk*, vn to work speedily (2. *modification* of the verb *alokamuk*, to work):

N'kezaloka, n'kezalokabena;	I work, we work, with celerity;
N'kezawighiga, n'keza-wighigabena.	He writes, they write, fast.

16. Neat working verb.—*Pabakalokamuk*, vn. to work neatly or carefully. (3. *modification* of the verb *alokamuk*, to work):

N'pabakaloka, n'paba-kalabena;	I work, we work, carefully;
'Pabakalokak.	They work carefully.

---

* This kind of verbs is called so, because they always indicate the *doing of a work,* that is, of the substantive from which it is derived, v. g. *ôgem,* snow shoe: *n'-d-ôgemika,* I make snow shoes; *ôwdi,* road: *n'-d-ôwdika,* I make a road.

17. Rough or coarse working verb.—*Mômôgualokamuk*, vn. to work roughly, (4. *modification* of the verb *alokamuk*, to work):

N'mômôgualoka, n'mô-môgualokabena;	I make, we make, rough or coarse work;
'Mômôgualokak.	They make coarse work

18. Conjunctive verb.—1. *Nisalokamuk*, to work two together; 2. *Kasalokamuk*, to work with someothers; 3. *Môwalokamuk*, to perform statute-labour or work many together, (*three* other modifications of the verb *alokamuk*, to work):

1. N'nisalokabena nijia.	I work with my brother, *or*, my brother and I work together.
2. N'kasaloka n'mitôgwes ta kedagik.	I work with my father *and* someothers.
3. N'môwalokabena *or* n'môwalokhedibena.	We perform statuate-labour; we all work together.

19. Feigning verb. *—*Akuamalsikôlzimuk*, vn. to feign to be sick. (Modification of the verb *akuamalsimuk*, to be sick).

(N'-d-akuamalsi.	I am sick).
N'-d-akuamalsikôlzi;	I feign to be sick.
'Akuamalsikôlzoak.	They feign to be sick.

20. Reproaching verb.—*Wazômawighigamuk*, vn., to write too much, (so to hurt oneself in one way or other). Modification of the verb *awighigamuk*, to write.

N'ozômawighiga, n'ozômawighigabena.	I write or wrote too much, we write or wrote too much (so that our sight is now weak).
'Wzômagighigak.	They write or wrote too much.

This means also: they wrote a *libellous* article.

---

* As in the Olchipwe Grammar, a verb of this kind represents always its subject doing something for show only, or by dissimulation.

21. Abundance verb.—*Masalawighôzik,* va. *masalawighigamuk,* vn. to write much. (*modification* of the verb, *awighôzik,* va., inanimate, and *awighigamuk,* vn., to write.

N'mesalawigham, n'mesalawighambena awighiganal.	I write, we write many letters.
'Msalawigham, msalawighamok awighi-	He writes, they write many letters.
N'mesalawighiga, n'mesalawighigabena;	I write much, we write much.
'Msalawighiga 'msala-wighigak.	He writes much, they write much.
(N'mesaladiali.	I made a good hunt).

22. Unipersonal-abundance verb.—This kind of verbs is formed from animate and inanimate substantives. No infinitive.

(*Moz,* moose;) mozika.	There is plenty of moose.
(*Pakesso,* partridge;) pakessoika.	There is plenty of partridges.
(*Abazi,* tree;) abazika.	There are many trees.
(*Sata,* blueberry;) sataika.	There is plenty of blueberries.

23. Unipersonal verb.—No infinitive.

Soglôn, soglônji.	It rains, it will rain.
Psôn, psônji.	It snows, it will snow.

24. Substantive verb.—*Sanôbaimuk,* to be a man; Sôjmôimuk, to be a chief, derived respectively from: *Sanôba,* a man, and *Sôgmô,* a chief.

N'sanôbai, n'sanôbai-bena, sôgmôibena;	I am a man, we are men; we are chiefs;
'Sanôbao, sôgmôo, sôgmôoak.	He is a man, he is a chief, they are chiefs.
(N'namasowi, 'namasoo, 'namasooak.	I am a fish, he is a fish, they are fish).

25. Adjective verb.—*Wôbigimuk*, to be white, derived from the adjective *wôbi*, white.

N'wôbigi, wôbigo, (wôbigen). | I am white, he is white, (it is white);
Wôbigoak, (wôbigenol). | They are white, (——things).
N'wizôwigi, wizôwigo, 'wizôwigoak. | I am yellow, he is yellow, they are yellow.

26. Possessive verbs.—*Wadôgemimuk*, to have snow shoes, *wadolimuk*, to have a canoe, derived from substantives, in the possessive case, *n'-d-ôgem*, my snow shoe; *n'dol*, my canoe:

N'odôgemi, 'wdôgemo, wdôgemoak. | I have snow shoes, he has snow shoes, they have snow shoes.
N'odoli, 'wdolo, 'wdoloak. | I have a canoe, he has a canoe, they have a canoe or canoes.

Note—These are not all the modifications which are to be observed in the Abenakis verb.

MISCELLANEOUS REMARKS

ON NOUNS, ADJECTIVES AND VERBS.

1. REMARKS.—Nouns being either *animale* or *inanimate*, it follows that there also *animate* and *inanimate* adjectives and verbs, which are made to agree with the nouns accordingly; and these nouns have therefore their respective *plural* termination, which are: *ak, ik, ok* and *k*, for the *animate*, and, *al, il, ol,* and *l*, for the *inanimate*. See page 17.

2. REMARK.—Generally the *diminutive* nouns are formed by the addition of *three* different terminations, viz: *s, is,* and *sis:*

(1) *Abazi*, a tree; *abazis*, a young tree; *sibo*, a river, *sibos*, a brook (or a narrow river).

(2) *Nebes* or *nbes*, a lake; *nebesis*, a small lake or pond; *sibos*, a brook; *sibosis*, a little brook; *wios*, some meat; *wiosis*, a small piece of meat.

(3) *Koa*, pine-tree; *koasis*, a young pine-tree; *abaznoda*, a basket; *abaznodasis*, a little basket; *sôgmô*, a chief; *sôgmôsis*, a small or young chief.

Nouns ending in *ôd, ad, at*, change their termination into *ôsid, asid, asit*, respectively: *nottahôd*, a butcher; *nottahôsid*, a small or young butcher; *nojikkad* a carpenter; *nojikkasid* a small or young carpenter; *soghebat*; an inn keeper; *soghebasit*, a small or young inn-keeper.

Nodatebit, a cook, makes: *nodalebesit*, a small or young cook; *notkuaag*, a pilot; *notkuaamosit*, a small or young pilot.

There is also the *extreme* diminutive, which is generally expressed by the annexation of *imis or simis* to the noun; as, *nebesimis*, a very small pond, a bog; *abaznodasimis*, a tiny little basket.

3. REMARK.—The *present* of the *indicative* is often used for the *future*; as:—

N'kwezoda kedak alemalokamuk, I will remove next week. (It ought to be: n'*kwezodaji*. . .)

N'môjibena siguaga, we will go away (*leave*) next spring.

The *past* is also often expressed by the *present*: as *n'namihô Salemen tagwôgua*, I have seen Salomon last fall; n'*nihlôbena moz siguana*, we have killed a moose last spring. (It ought to be: *n'kizi nhlôbena*. . .)

4. REMARK.—*Should* and *would* are always expressed by *ba* affixed to the verb, (see congutation); but when *should* is used for *ought*, then

should is expressed by *achowiba*, the equivalent of *ought*, placed between the pronoun and the verb; as:

K'-d-achowiba majimiwi kdemôgalmônna kademôksessit, we should always asssist the poor.

The *potential* is expressed by *kiziba*, placed before the verb; as thus: *n'kiziba mezenemenana*, we might have it (get it); *k'kiziba ôbankawô*, you might pay him.

5. REMARK.—The *interrogative* conjugation has been omitted in this book, because any sentence, be it *affirmative* or *negative*, may become *interrogative*, if only you change the usual *affirmative* tune into an *interrogative*, or, in writing, end the sentence by the *interrogation* point (?); as in the following sentences:

K'-d-awigham awighigan, you write a letter;
K'-d-awigham awighigan? do you write a letter?
N'môjibena Sandaga, we will start Sunday;
Nmôjibena Sandaga? shall we start Sunday?
O'da k'-d-agakimziw, you do not study;
O'da k'-d-agakimziw? don't you study?

ETYMOLOGY

OF INDIAN NAMES BY WHICH ARE DESIGNATED CERTAIN TRIBES, TOWNS, RIVERS, LAKES, ETC., ETC.

B efore commencing this treatise, it would perhaps be well to mention that all these names, either in Abenakis, Cree or other tribal languages, which now designate so many localities, mountains, rivers, etc., have been so much disfigured by the *Whites*, who not understanding these words, pronounced them in the best way they could and spelled them accordingly, but, in most cases, with such incorrectness that they have rendered many of them altogether incomprehensible, and thereby impossible to discover their true signification.

ABENAKIS, (Abenakis), from: "Wôbanaki," land or country of the East. This name comes from: *wôban*, daybreak, and, *ki*, earth, land, or rather, *aki*, which is a term employed in composition for, land, ground, region. *Wôbanaki*, Abenakis, means also: an Indian from where the daylight comes. The *plur.* makes: *wôbanakiak.*

ACHIGAN, probably from: *Manashigan*, (Cree), or Mônazigan, (Abenakis), a fish that the French people have named "achigan", and the English, "black bass."

ALSIGÔNTEGW, (Abenakis), is the name given to the River St-Francis, by the Indians of this tribe. It means: river abounding in shells; hence the modern name: *Alsigôntegwiak*, the Indians of St-Francis.

ALNÔBAI Menahan, (Abenakis), Indian Island, is an island owned by the Abenakis, situated in the River St-Francis, two miles below the Indian village. The *whites* call that island: "He Ronde," round island.

AMONOOSUC, (Abenakis), from, *O'manosek*, the fishing ground, or better, the small or narrow fishing river. Some pretend that it comes from: *pagônozik*, at the walnut-tree, from *pagônozi*, walnut-tree.

ANNAPOLIS River; *Tawapskak*, flowing out between rocks.

AROOSTOOK, (Abenakis), from *Walastegw*, shallow river, or perhaps, *Wlastegw*, good river.

ASAWABIMOSWAN, (Cree), where hunters watch for the elk.

ATTAKAPAS, probably from: *Adagôbas*, rogue, roguish man. This word is sometimes used in figurative sense, and then it means: man-eater.

ATTIKAMIGUES, (Cree), for *attikamek*, white fish.

ARTHABASKA, (Abenakis), from, *albataika*, or rather, *albataska*, there are many putrid water places or swamps, from: *albata* or *albatas*, putrid water, and *ka* or *ika*, an Abenakis *suffix* marking abundance.

BATISCAN, (in Abenakis, "Padiskôn") probably for, Baptist's camp. Padoskan, signifies: one makes a boat (or boats).

BASKANEGAN, (Abenakis), "Poskenigan," coffin. (*poskeniganiko*, a grave yard). It was likely a place where the Indians, in old times, used to bury their dead. Burial was performed by placing a hewed tomb upon a scaffold in which were placed the remains of the deceased, with all is hunting accoutrements, ammunution and dried meat.

BECANCOUR, "Wôlinaktegw," the river which has long turns, or rather which causes delay by its windings.

BELŒIL MOUNTAIN, (St-Hilaire); Wigwômadensis, (*sis*) a diminutive term: Mountain resembling to (or in the form of) a *wigwam*. Hence the local term: "Wigwômadesisek," which is the name given to the city of St-Hyacinthe by the Abenakis Indians.

BLACK RIVER, *Mkazawi Sibo*, (black river).

BLUE MOUNTAINS, Yar. Co., N. S., named in Abenakis *Walôwadenik*, (bl. mts.), are called in Micmac: *Cookwejook*, the spectres.

BEAR ISLAND, (Lake Winnipesaukee,) Awasoswi Menahan.

CANADA, from, *Kanata*, (Iroquois), a collection of tents or huts.

CANSO, (Micmac), *camsok*, opposite a high bluff.

CASCUMPEK; *Caskamkek*, (Micmac), a bold steep sandy shore.

CAPE MISPEC: *Masbaak*, (Abenakis); *Mespaak*, (Micmac), over-flowed.

CHICOUTIMI, (Abenakis), *Saguitemik*, where it is deep by the act of the sea tide; *Saguitema*, it is deep by the act of the tide.

CHAWINIGAN, (Abenakis), *Azawinigan*, bold-steep (roof-like) portage. Some pretend that it is derived from *Shâwan* or *Sâwan*, (Cree) south, and, *onigan*, portage.

COHASSET, probably for: *koasek*, the young pine-tree. *Koa*, means pine-tree. *Koas* is the diminutive, and, *koasek*, the local term.

COCOCACHE, (Abenakis), for, *kokokhas*, an owl; the local term: *kokokhasek*. This is the name of a lake on the St Maurice River, about 150 miles above Three Rivers, which is so called on account of a little mountain, at the East-end of the lake, the form of which, especially the extreme top, resembles an owl.

CONNECTICUT, (Abenakis), for: *Kwenitegw* (or *Kwunitukw*), long river. The local term, is: *Kwenitegok*.

CAUGHNAWAGA, (Iroquois), for, *kahnawake*, at the falls, from: *ka*, where, *ohnawa*, current, swift current, falls, cascade, and *ke*, which marks: 1° the duality and plurality; 2° the presence of a preposition, which, in many instances, (in the Indian languages,) is represented by the termination.

COHOES, probably for: *koas*, young pine, or perhaps *koasek*, at the young pine-tree.

COOKSAKEE, (Abenakis), from, *skok* or *skog*, snake, and, *aki*, or *ki*, land: snake land.

COATICOOK, (Abenakis), comes from the local term: *Koatteg'ok*, at the Pine River, derived from: *Koa*, pine-tree, *ttegw*, river, (in composition only), and the suffix *ok* which has the force of either of these prepositions: *at, lo, of, from, on, in.*

CHENAL-DU-MOINE is designated by the Abenakis Indians under the name of "*Poltegw*," which means: *Paul's River.*

CHAMOCHA, a clown; a masked man.

DACOTAH, (Ind.), leagued; allied, the common name of the confederate Sioux tribes. (*National Stand Dictionary*, 537).

DAHLONEGA, (Ind.), place of gold. (*Nat Stand. Dictionary*).

DAMARISCOTTA, (Ind.) alewife place. (*N. Stand. Dictionary*).

DEVIL'S ROCK; *Madahôndoapskw*, (Abenakis), *Mundoopscoochk*, (Micmac), devil's rock.

DURHAM, (L'Avenir,) is called by the Abenakis: Kwanahômoik: where the turn of the river makes a long point.

ESQUIMAUX, a tribe that the Abenakis name: *Askimo*, plur. *askimoak*, eaters of raw flesh.

ERIE, said to be the name of a fierce tribe exterminated by the Iroquois. (*National Stand. Dictionary*).

ESCOUMINS, (Cree), from *iskomin*, from *isko* till there, and *min*, berry, that is, there are berries till such a place (*Gramm. of the Olchipwe language*, 298)

ETCHEMIN, (Ochipwe) from *iyekomin*, from *iyeko*, sand, and *min*, berry, or sand-berries, so the Otchipw indians call raspberries.

FORD ELLIS, *Mâdawaak*, (Micmac), *Paskategwak*, (Abenakis), where the river branches off.

THE FALLS, *Câpskw*, (Micmac), *Panjahlôk* (Abenakis), a cascade. *Pôntegw* means equally, cascade, falls.

THE GRAND FALLS, *Kchi Pôntegw*, (Abenakis), grand falls; local term: *Kchi Pôntegok*, at the great falls.

FRENCH RIVER, *Plachmôni Sibo.* (Abenakis).

FIVE ISLANDS, *Nankûl mûnegool,* (Micmac); *Nonnenagak,* (Abenakis) at the five islands; (idiomatic: *nônnenagol,* the five islands, lit: *nônnowigil menahanol*).

FOX ISLAND, *Wôkwsesi menahan,* (Abenakis). In local term: *Wôkwesi meuahanok.*

GATINEAU RIVER; *Madôbajoak,* (Abenakis), the river which flows rapidly into another.

GRAND LAKE, N. B., *Kchi nebes,* (Abenakis); *Tûlûgadik,* (Micmac), camping ground.

GRAND MANAN; *manan* is probably from, *manahan,* (Abenakis), island, which, being connected with "grand," makes: "grand island."

GRAND RIVER is, in Abenakis, *Kchi sibo,* (lit. meaning).

GRINDSTONE BANK, *keedâkûnûk,* (Micmac), *kitadôganapskw,* (Abenakis), whetstone rock.

HAYTI, (Ind.) high land. (*Nat. Stand. dictionary*).

HERON ISLAND; (Abenakis), *Kaskoi menahan.*

HOUSATONIC, (Abenakis), for *awasadenik,* beyond the mountain; over the hill. This is from: *awasi...* beyond, *aden,* mountain or hill (only in composition), and *ik,* one of the Abenakis suffixes which gives the name in local term.

ILLINOIS, from *ilini,* (Algonquin), man, and the French addition *ois,* for tribe or people, or rather from, *iliniwok,* men or "band of men".

IOWA, the French form of an Indian word, signifying "the drowsy" or "the sleepy ones"; a Sioux name of the Pahoja or "Gray snow tribe," (*Nat. Stand. Dictionary*).

IGLISMÔNKI, (Abenakis), England, (*lit*; Englishman's land).

ILLÔDAKKI, (Abenakis), Ireland, (*lit*: Irishman's land).

IGLISMÔN, (Abenakis), Englishman; English people. The English militia, *makwsawat,* (*lit. signification*: who wears a red uniform).

KAANAWAGI, the name by which the Abenakis designate the Indian Reserve of the Iroquois tribe, known under the name of Caughnawaga.

KAANAWAGIHNONO, (Abenakis), the Iroquois tribe of Caughnawaga.

KAMOURASKA, probably from, *ska môraskua* (old Abenakis), *ska môlaskua,* (modern expression), there is some white birch bark, or perhaps for: there are some white birch trees.

KANSAS, probably from: *Kanosas,* which means, willow.

KATAHDIN, (Abenakis), for *Ktaden*, the big or high mountain.

KEARSARGE, probably from: *Kesarzet*, (old Abenakis), the proud or selfish.

KÉNÉBEC, (Abenakis), for, *Kinebek*, or *Kinebak*, large lake, or again, deep river.

KIWAKUAI SIBO, *Cannibal River*, a branch of the St-Maurice River. *Kiwakua*, (Abenakis), man-eater.

KWANÔBAGNAGAK, or *Kwanôbagnagasik*, (diminutive), is the name given by the Abenakis to a little island owned by them, on the river St-Francis, known under the name of "L'Ile-à-l'Ail." It means: long narrow island.

KENOSHA, probably for: *Kwenoza*, (Abenakis), pike.

KWENOSASEK, (Abenakis idiom), means: at the pike river.

KENTUCKY, likely for, *Kwenataga*, it is long.

KOATTEGOK, (Abenakis), local term of *koattegw*, pine river. See *Coaticook*.

MADÔBALODENIK, an idiomatical expression by which the Abenakis designate the city of Three Rivers, after the former name of the River St Maurice, which was: *Lodenoi sibo*. It was so called, because in old times, when the hunting territories were all devided among the Indians, this river, from its mouth up to a certain distance, belonged to an indian named *Lodeno*. The expression *madôbalodenik*, from: *madôba***ik*, which comes or flows in, and the interposition of *loden*, an abbreviation of *Lodeno*, means: the outlet or confluence of the *River Lodeno*.

MACKINAW, probably from: *mikenakw*, (Abenakis), a tortoise; also, a species of waterbug.

MACCAN RIVER; *Mââgan*, (Micmac), fishing place.

MADAWASKA; *matawaska*, (Otchipwe), *madôbaskika*, (Abenakis), the mouth of a river where there are grass and hay. The local term is *madôbaskikak*.

MAKUAPSKASIK, (Abenakis), is the name of a short portage, on the St Francis River, above the Abenakis village, which means: at the red rock.

MAMPHREMAGOG, (Abenakis), for, *Mamlawbagak*, signifies; long and large sheet of water, from: *mamlaw...*, a prefix which denotes largeness or abundance, *baga*, a particule denoting water, and, *k*, which marks that the name is given in local term.

MASKIKOWOGAMAK, (Abenakis), the lake the banks of which are covered with grass or hay.

MASKUAANAGASIK, (Abenakis), the diminutive of *maskuaanagak:* the little birch-trees island, or simply, the birch island. This is the name of a little island on the River St Francis.

MASSACHUSETTS, either from: "Massajosets," the tribe of the great hill, or, *Msajosek,* at the great hill or region of the great hills.

MANHATTAN, (Abenakis), from: *menahanilan,* an island formed by the current or the tide.

MANITOLINE, for: *manito w-d-ain,* the spirit (manito) is there, or, *manito l'île,* (half Indian and French), the manito island.

MANTAWA or Matawin, (Abenakis), junction of two rivers.

MERRIMACK, from the old Abenakis, *Morôdemak,* deep river.

MICHILIMACKINAC, (Abenakis), probably from: *msalmikenakw,* there is plenty of turtles.

MILWAUKEE, (Abenakis), probably for: *milwai ki,* fertile *or* productive land.

MEGANTIC, (Abenakis), for: *namakôttik,* or rather, *namagwôttik,* (old Abenakis), which means, lake trout place.

MISTASSINI, the big stone.

MATAPEDIAC; (Abenakis), *madôbajoak,* a river flowing roughly into another.

MALPEQUE, (Micmac) *mâkpââk,* said to mean, big bay.

MISSISSIPI, great or grand river.

MONADNOCK, according to the Abenakis orthography, *môniadenok,* or *mônadenok,* (elliptical), signifies: at the silver mountain, from: *môni,* silver, *aden,* mountain, and the termination *ok,* which has the force of either of these prepositions: *at, to, of, from, on.*

MISSISQUOI, comes from: *Masipskoik,* (Abenakis), where there is flint.

MOOSEHEAD LAKE, is called in Abenakis: *Mozodupi Nebes,* which is the literal meaning of the English name.

MANAWAN (Lake), eggs gathering place. In fact, that lake being the resort of gulls and loons, the hunters use to gather lots of eggs around the little islands.

NASHUA is said to mean: between (the rivers). *Between* is expressed in Abenakis by: *nsawi, nsawiwi* or *nansawiwi.*

NIKATTEGW *or* Nikôntegw, (Abenakis), means: first branch, or again, the outrunning stream or river. This is the Indian name of a channal, at the lower end of the Abenakis Indian Reserve of St-Francis called by the French people "Chenal Tardif."

NIAGARA, probably from, *Ohniara*, (Iroquois), the neck (connecting Lake Erie with Lake Ontario).

NAMAGWÔTTIK, (Abenakis), place abounding in lake trout. (*See Megantic*).

O'BAMAS, a term by which the Abenakis Indians designate the "Rivière du Loup" (en haut), means: opposite course or winding. This name has been given on account of the great winding which commences a little bellow Hunters town Mills. See plan of the St-Maurice Territory, published in 1857.

O'BAMASIS, the diminutive of *O'bamas*, is the name given by the Abenakis to the "River Yamachiche."

O'BÔMKAIK is the name by which la "Pointe-du-Lac" is designated by the Abenakis. It means: the white sandy point.

O'NKOBAGAK, (Abenakis,) lake lengthened or extended after a strait.

ONEIDA, (Ind.), people of the beacon stone (*National Stand. Dictionary*).

ONTARIO, from Onontee, "a village on a mountain," the chief seat of the Onondagas, (*N. S. Dictionary*).

OSWEGO, the Onondaga name for Lake Ontario, (*N. S. Dictionary*).

OUIATCHOAN, (Crree), from, *wûwiyâtjiwan*, or *wayawitjiwan*, currunt coming out.

OTTAWA, perhaps from, *otonwa*, (Iroquois), beaver's lodge, muskrat's lodge. The Otchipwe grammar says, however, that it is an abbreviation of: *ottawakay*, his ear, or, *otawask*, and *watawask*, bull-rushes, because along the river there are a great many of those bull-rushes, while A. L. Burt's N. S. Dictionary states that it means, *traders*.

PASSUMPSIC, probably from: *pasômkasik*, (Abenakis), a diminutive term which means: river which has a clear sandy bottom.

PAWCATUCK, (Abenakis), shaking river, or perhaps from, *pôgwkategw*, the shallow river.

PAWTUCKET, probably from, *pawtagit*, (Abenakis), who shakes himself, which shakes itself: a figurative sense applied sometimes to falls.

PICHOUX, (Abenakis), *pezo*, (Cree), *pisiw*, lynx.

PITHIGAN, (Abenakis), the entry, inlet, opening, of a river or lake.

PITHIGANITEGW is the name by which the Abenakis designate the River Nicolet.

PEMIGEWASSET, (Abenakis), comes from: *Pamijowasik*, diminutive of *pamijowak*, which means, the swift or rapid current; *pamijowasik*, the narrow and shallow swift current.

Piscataqua, (Ind.), great deer river. (*Nat. Stand. Dictionary*).

Potomac, (Ind.), place of the burning pine, resembling a council-fire. (*N. S. Dictionary*).

Penobscot, probably from: *pamapskak,* (Abenakis), the rocky place, among the rocks, or perhaps from: *panapskak,* the steep rocky place.

Quebec, from the old Abenakis, *Kebhek* or *Kebek,* means: obstructed current; where it is narrow or shut.

Quinebaug, (Abenakis), for, *Kwanbaak,* long pond.

Rimouski, (old Abenakis), *Aremoski,* (modern), *Alemoski,* means, dog's land, from: *aremos* or *alemos,* dog, and, *ki,* land or country.

Sagaswantegw, half Algonquin and Abenakis, *sagaswa,* (Alg.), he is smoking, and, *tegw,* (Ab.), river, given in figurative sense, for: still river, that is, river where one has ample time to smoke.

Saranac (Ind.) is said to mean: river that flows under rock.

Saratoga, (ind.), place of the miraculous water in a rock. (*Nat. Stand. Dictionary*). The Abenakis Indians designate this place by *nebizonbik,* a local term, which means: at the mineral spring, or rather, at the physical water.

Saskatchewan, (Cree), *saskijoan,* (Abenakis): rapid current.

Schoodic, probably from the old Abenakis, *skudek,* at the fire, or, burnt lands, (from large fires about 1675).

Sebago, probably from, *sobagoo,* (Abenakis), it is sea, or, it resembles a sea.

Seneca, (Abenakis), *senika,* means; there are many rocks, it is rocky, from: *sen,* rock, stone, and *ika,* an addition which marks abundance. (*Môni,* money; *môniika,* there is plenty of money).

Sisikwai Menahan, (Abenakis), rattlesnake island.

Sisiquoi, perhaps for, *sisikwa,* rattlesnake.

Skowhegan, (Abenakis), from *skuahigen,* or *skwahigen,* it is pointed.

Saco, is believed to come from *sok8ai,* (old Abenakis), which means: from the South side; Southern. Hence the name *sok8aki,* (modern, *sokoki*), Southern country; Southern people, or better, Indians from the South.

Saguenay River is called by the *Micmacs* "Ktadoosôk", flowing between two high steep cliffs.

St John, N. B., (Micmac), *Mènawgès,* where they collect the dead seals.

Suncook, (Abenakis), from *senikok,* at the rocks.

Tennessee, (Ind.), river of the Big Bend (*N. S. Dictionary*).

TADOUSSAC, (Cree), from, *totosak* plural of *tôtôs,* woman's breast pap. (*Otchip. gramm*).

TEMISCOUATA, it is deep everywhere, from, *timiw,* it is deep in the water, and, *iskwatâm* without end (*Otchip. gramm*).

UMBAGOG, (Ind.) clear lake, shallow. (*N. S. Dictionary*).

WACHUSETT, (Abenakis) from, *wajos,* a mountain (of middling height), and the *prepositive* termination *ek,* which represents the preposition *at*: at the mountain.

WABISHTONIS, (Och.), from *wabistânis,* diminutive of *wabistân,* a marten.

WASHITA, (Western Indian language), said to mean: a buck, a male deer.

WASSABAASTEGW, (Abenakis) white river; clear water stream.

WDAMÔGANASPSKOK, (Abenakis), a name by which is designated a rapid on the River St-Francis, which means: at the pipe rock.

WDUPSEK, (Abenakis), an expression signifying: a scalping spot, at the crown.

WIGWÔM, wigwâm, a house, a lodge.

WINNIPEG, unpure *or* turbid water, salt water.

WINNEPESAUKEE *or* Winnipisiogee (Abenakis), comes from: *Wiwininebesaki,* lake in the vicinity of which there are other lakes and ponds, or perhaps better, lake region, from: *wiwni,* abbreviation of *wiwniwi,* around, in the vicinity, *nebes,* lake, pond, and, *aki,* land, rigion, territory.

WINOOSKI, (Abenakis), from *winos,* onion, and, *ki,* land: *Winoski,* onion land.

WAWÔBADENIK, (Abenakis), White Mountains, N. H. The "Mount Washington" is called in Abenakis "Kôdaakwajo," the hidden mountain, so called because in cloudy weather the top of that mountain, owing to its great elavation, is, in fact, always hidden by the clouds.

WISCASSUT, is said to mean, at the yellow pines:

WASHITA, (Western Indian language), said to mean, a buck, a male deer.

WASSABAASTEGW, (Abenakis) white river, clear water stream.

WABASKOUTIYUNK (Lake) is said to mean in Montagnais: where there is some whitish grass or hay.

SIGNIFICATION

OF THE NAMES OF THE MONTHS.

January; *Alamikos*;
New-year's greeting month.
February; *Piaôdagos*;
Boughs-shedding month.
March; *Mozokas*;
Moose-hunting month.
April; *Sogalikas*;
Sugar-making month.
May; *Kikas*;
Planting month.
June; *Nokkahigas*;
Hoeing month.
July; *Temaskikos*;
Hay-making month.
August; *Temezôwas*;
Harvesting month.
September; *Skamonkas*;
Indian corn-reaping month.
October; *Penibagos*;
Leaf-falling month.
November; *Mzatanos*;
Ice-forming month.
December; *Pebonkas*;
Winter month.

ABENAKIS CHIEF JOSEPH LAURENT

A Note About the Author

Joseph Laurent (1839-1917) was an Abenaki Chief, author, entrepreneur and teacher. While Laurent is known for leading the Abenaki reserve of Odanak as well as establishing a trading post in Interval, New Hampshire, he is most-recognized as the author of New Familiar Abenakis and English Dialogues. Published in 1884, the book would serve as Laurent's crowning achievement—being the first dictionary to translate the Abenaki language to English as well as being one of the first literary productions of the Abenaki tribe in general.

A Note from the Publisher

Spanning many genres, from non-fiction essays to literature classics to children's books and lyric poetry, Mint Edition books showcase the master works of our time in a modern new package. The text is freshly typeset, is clean and easy to read, and features a new note about the author in each volume. Many books also include exclusive new introductory material. Every book boasts a striking new cover, which makes it as appropriate for collecting as it is for gift giving. Mint Edition books are only printed when a reader orders them, so natural resources are not wasted. We're proud that our books are never manufactured in excess and exist only in the exact quantity they need to be read and enjoyed.

bookfinity™

Discover more of your favorite classics with Bookfinity™.

- Track your reading with custom book lists.
- Get great book recommendations for your personalized Reader Type.
- Add reviews for your favorite books.
- AND MUCH MORE!

Visit **bookfinity.com** and take the fun Reader Type quiz to get started.

Enjoy our classic and modern companion pairings!

Classic & Modern

Printed in the USA
CPSIA information can be obtained
at www.ICGtesting.com
JSHW022147211123
52507JS00002B/17